OUT OF THE
BLUE

BOISE STATE

Undefeated Fiesta Bowl Champions

THE ARBITER

*arbiter*online.com

StanleyBrewster
FOTO2O8.COM

SP
SPORTS
PUBLISHING
L.L.C.

SportsPublishingLLC.com

SportsPublishingLLC.com

PUBLISHERS
PETER L. BANNON AND
JOSEPH J. BANNON SR.

SENIOR MANAGING EDITOR
SUSAN M. MOYER

EDITOR
LAURA E. PODESCHI

ART DIRECTOR
JEFF HIGGERSON

COVER DESIGNER
JOSEPH T. BRUMLEVE

PHOTO EDITOR
ERIN LINDEN-LEVY

BOOK LAYOUT
LAURA E. PODESCHI
JEFF HIGGERSON

IMAGING
DUSTIN J. HUBBART
JEFF HIGGERSON

THE ARBITER
*arbiter*online.com

StanleyBrewster
FOTO208.COM

AUTHORS
JAKE GARCIN: SPORTS EDITOR
KYE JOHNSON: ASSISTANT SPORTS EDITOR
JESSICA CHRISTENSEN: NEWS EDITOR
DUSTIN LAPRAY: MANAGING EDITOR
DREW MAYES: EDITOR-IN-CHIEF

ADVISORS
BRAD ARENDT: GENERAL MANAGER
DR. DAN MORRIS: EDITORIAL ADVISOR

COPY EDITOR
SHEREE WHITELEY: LEAD COPY EDITOR

PHOTOGRAPHY
STANLEY BREWSTER: PHOTOGRAPHER

ISBN 10: 1-59670-271-0
ISBN 13: 978-1-59670-271-4

Front cover photos: Petersen photo by Jonathan Ferrey/Getty Images;
   background photo by Stanley Brewster/Arbiter.
Back cover photo: Stanley Brewster/Arbiter.

Sports Publishing L.L.C.
804 North Neil Street
Champaign, IL 61820
Phone: 1-877-424-2665
Fax: 217-363-2073
SportsPublishingLLC.com

Printed in the United States of America.

CONTENTS

Editor's Note   4

Preseason   8

Game 1: Sacramento State   14

Profile: Drisan James   20

Profile: Jared Zabransky   24

Game 2: Oregon State   28

Game 3: at Wyoming   34

Profile: Chris Petersen   40

Game 4: Hawaii   44

Game 5: at Utah   50

Game 6: Louisiana Tech   56

Game 7: at New Mexico State   64

Game 8: at Idaho   70

Game 9: Fresno State   76

Profile: Ian Johnson   82

Game 10: at San Jose State   86

Game 11: Utah State   92

Game 12: at Nevada   98

Profile: Korey Hall   104

Profile: Jeff and Pete Cavender   108

Fiesta Bowl: vs. Oklahoma   112

Season Stats   124

EDITOR'S NOTE

BREAKING THROUGH THE GLASS CEILING

Drew Mayes, Editor-in-Chief
The Arbiter

What a year for the Boise State Broncos!

After starting the season off as an unranked team, the Broncos rose to the upper echelon of college football in 2006—becoming just the second non-Bowl Championship Series conference team to reach a BCS game.

Despite the lack of preseason hype and national respect, the team 'kept it rolling' on its way to the second undefeated regular season in three years in typical, dominating Bronco fashion.

The season started with myriad questions and *The Arbiter* was there from the beginning to get you the answers.

Could the team continue its success under a rookie head coach?

Would two coordinators who hadn't even seen their 30th birthdays at the start of the season be ready for that type of responsibility?

After a disappointing and controversial junior year, how would the Broncos' senior quarterback perform with all eyes on him?

Was the program ready to handle its first Heisman candidate?

We learned the answers to these questions and more throughout the season and now so can you. Turn these pages to relive the greatest season in the history of Boise State football, including a game-by-game recap.

Following the team throughout the 2006 season has been an incredible adventure for us at *The Arbiter* and we're happy to share it with you.

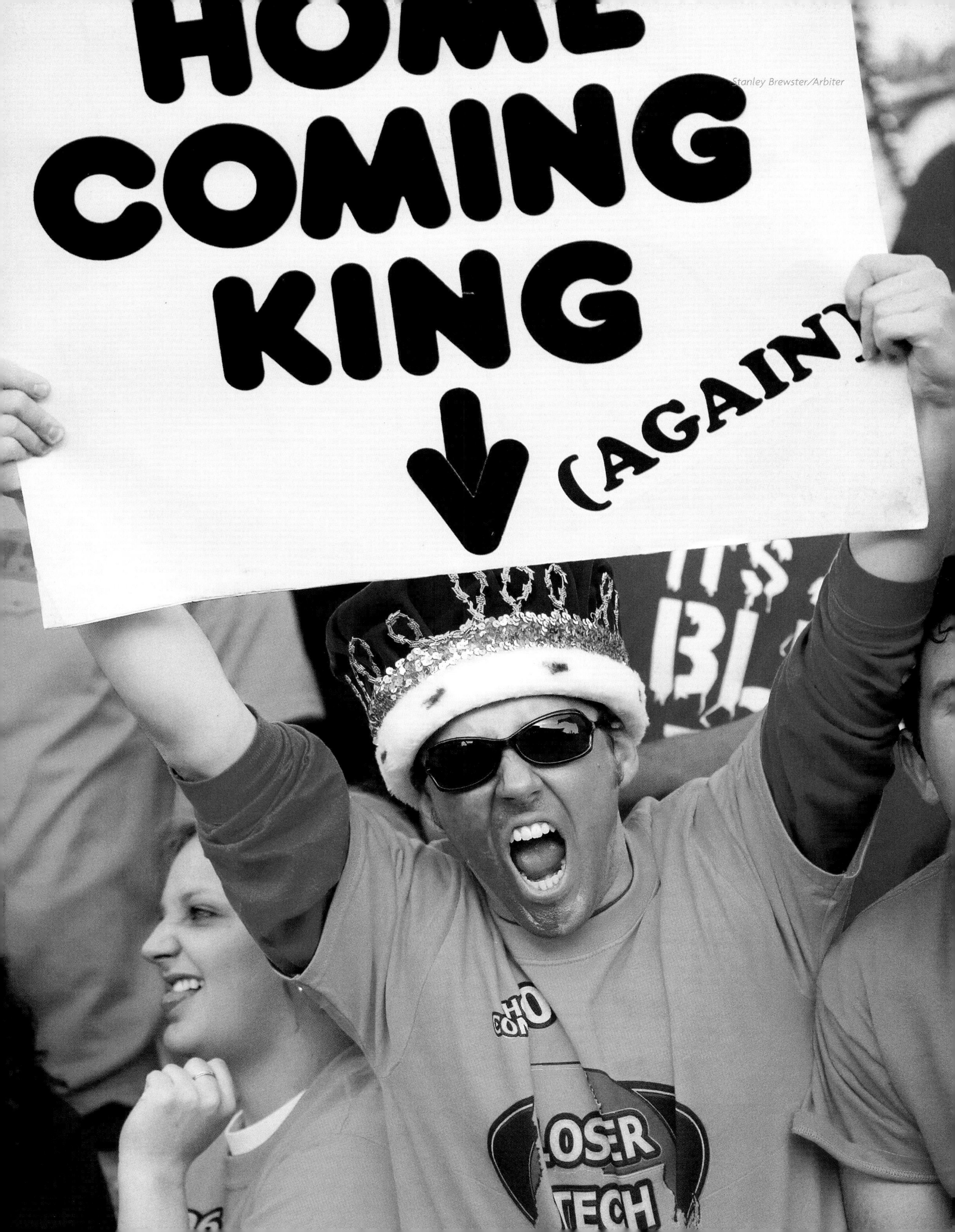

Stanley Brewster/Arbiter

BRONCOS HOLD FINAL SCRIMMAGE

BY DUSTIN LAPRAY

It wasn't anything spectacular, earth-shaking. But it was clean and it got the fans out of their seats.

Those fans got their glimpse of the Boise State football squad on a Friday night at the team's final open fall scrimmage. The Broncos will scrimmage once more, but that is closed to the public and the media.

BSU head coach Chris Petersen held out a handful of his starters, to give them rest and keep them healthy.

"This is the last time that some of the young guys are really going to get a chance to play (in front of any people at least) so we wanted to give those guys a good shot," Petersen said.

In all, the team only scored 17 points, but put together some long drives and featured a much-improved game by senior starter Jared Zabransky.

Zabransky scored one of the Broncos' two touchdowns on a one-yard sneak. He rushed for 45 yards on eight carries in the scrimmage.

Ashlei Nyong-Dunham (29) tackles Julian Hawkins (82) during the Blue and Orange scrimmage.
Stanley Brewster/Arbiter

"(Zabransky) has been doing a great job in camp," Petersen said. "He's a weapon. He's got to be one of the faster QBs in the country in terms of his foot speed. If he can continue to make good, smart decisions, with that foot speed we'll be in good shape."

Zabransky also went 7-of-14 through the air for 95 yards in his limited action.

"I think he's being smart," Petersen said. "He has to be two things: an accurate thrower and a good decision maker. He's been working on that for a year solid and you can see his decisions are getting better. He's not going to be perfect, nobody is, but as long as we're making progress and getting better, we're happy with that."

Zabransky was perhaps shown up again by backups Bush Hamdan (3-for-3, 100 yards) and Nick Lomax (6-for-7, 91 yards, TD).

Zabransky has a bad habit of tucking the ball after his first read on the defense and running downfield. But he is making better decisions. Rather than risking a loss or throwing a bad pass, like he may have done in the past, the senior has learned to throw the ball out of bounds when needed.

"He still likes to think he's Brett Favre on occasion and fire that ball in there," Petersen said. "He's doing a good job, being a smart QB, knowing when to run and when to throw it out of bounds and when to take a shot in there."

Lomax threw the game's only touchdown pass, a 25-yard drifter, which floated into the

> "I STRUGGLED A COUPLE OF DAYS IN PRACTICE. THEN I CAME OUT ON TOP AND SHOWED UP AT THE SCRIMMAGE. THAT WAS A GOOD THING."
>
> BSU WIDE RECEIVER AIONA KEY

open arms of freshman receiver Aiona Key.

"I struggled a couple of days in practice," Key (6-foot-4, 194 lbs.) said. "Then I came out on top and showed up at the scrimmage. That was a good thing."

Key was the highlight and the standout in the scrimmage, hauling in five catches for 108 yards.

"Aiona is a phenomenal athlete," Petersen said. "He really is. We're trying to figure out a way to get him on the field, we put him in on defense there at the end too. We're trying to make him a special team phenom. We're really trying to figure out how to get him on the field; he does make plays."

Key is part of a very deep receiving corps and probably won't get a starting spot, but he really wants a spot, any spot.

"If you ask any player, it would mean a lot (to start for BSU)," Key said. "Everybody on the team is really good, so if you can beat out another guy, that means you are really, really good."

Legedu Naanee, Drisan James, Jerard Rabb, and Jeremy Childs are all on the depth chart ahead of Key. Friday may have been his best opportunity to catch the limelight. But Petersen

Quarterback Jared Zabransky looks for a receiver during the annual scrimmage.
Stanley Brewster/Arbiter

10

will find a role for him, whether he plays safety or special teams, the man will take the field.

During the scrimmage, the Broncos worked on the backed-up offense and backed-up defense packages, designed to teach the team what it would be like to have that pressure in front of a crowd.

"WE'RE NOT THERE YET, BUT WE WILL BE IN TWO WEEKS."

BSU HEAD COACH CHRIS PETERSEN

The team also worked on all of its special teams, including punts (two of which were blocked, one returned for a touchdown by Austin Smith). The Bronco longsnapper, Mike Dominguez, had troubles with high snaps, but Petersen said he'd have that locked down. Dominguez has been the longsnapper for two years.

Overall, the Broncos looked good. They had fewer penalties, and the defense is the main reason the offense can't get it going.

"We're not there yet, but we will be in two weeks," Petersen said. "We've got a lot of work left to do. We're now moving into the very much detailed phase of our offense and defense. We'll start bearing down and get into our two-deep stuff and then we'll start game planning."

The Broncos did get to work some of their situational plays.

"We tried to do a little backed-up offense and defense and do a little goalline," Petersen said. "It's important to practice those things when we get some more people in the stands. It changes the kids' anxiety level. The more we can do those type of things, situational things, the better for us."

The Broncos are working through a few injury problems. Andrew Woodruff, the starting right tackle on offense, left the scrimmage with a leg injury, but Petersen said he would be fine. The Broncos have a lot of depth at certain positions, but have scattered depth at running back and in the defensive backfield.

"We feel okay right now," Petersen said. "But we can't keep losing guys like we have. Soon we will run out of that depth. You hate to lose anybody, at any position. If we can stay healthy from here on out, we'll be fine."

The Broncos open the season against Sacramento State August 31 at Bronco Stadium.

Running back Quinton Jones picks up yardage during the Blue and Orange Game. *Stanley Brewster/Arbiter*

BRONCOS STING HORNETS 45-0

BY JAKE GARCIN

Eight months worth of questions were erased in one single play August 31 after an Ian Johnson touchdown that acted as an official introduction to 2006 Bronco football. On Boise State's first offensive drive of the game, a 19-yard touchdown run by Johnson electrified Bronco Stadium, giving new head coach Chris Petersen's squad a spark that would propel them into overdrive for the first 15 minutes of the game.

The first Bronco score came just 4:26 into the contest on a five-play opening drive, which gave way to two more rushing touchdowns in the first quarter. Senior quarterback Jared Zabransky found the end zone on a one-yard sneak up the middle at the 5:10 mark, shortly followed by a second Johnson touchdown with 2:46 still to play in the first. The score came on a four-yard punch that gave Johnson 61 yards rushing on just eight carries in the quarter.

The fast Boise State start was due in large part to BSU's control over the line of scrimmage early on. BSU's quick success on the ground also gave way to a more wide-open passing approach in the quarters to follow. Zabransky found Legedu Naanee for a three-yard touchdown pass on the opening drive of the second quarter, giving BSU a 28-0 halftime lead over the Hornets.

Linebacker Korey Hall (25) and the Boise State defense take down Hornets running back Kris Daniels. *Stanley Brewster/Arbiter*

Sacramento State defensive back Durrell Oliver gets a hand on the pass intended for Boise State receiver Jeremy Childs.

Stanley Brewster/Arbiter

It took only 2:40 for the Broncos to strike again in the second half, when Zabransky found wide receiver Drisan James on a 52-yard hook up down the heart of the Sacramento State defense. An Anthony Montgomery field goal from 33 yards out in the third and a one-yard Jon Helmandollar touchdown run with 1:18 left in the game sealed Sacramento State's fate, falling 45-0 to the overpowering Bronco attack.

The Broncos were able to amass 215 yards on the ground against the Hornets. Johnson led the way with 89 rushing yards on just 13 carries for the game. BSU did manage to balance out the attack in the later quarters, tallying 212 yards in the air. Zabransky completed 11 of 20 passes for 181 yards in just over three quarters of work. Zabransky gave a great deal of credit to his offensive line after the game, for making the offensive push possible.

"We knew what we needed to get done," Zabransky said. "You know a large part of that was execution. The first few times we touched the ball we moved it down the field and put it in the end zone. I felt very comfortable back there. It's easy to feel comfortable when you've got a great offensive line like we do, and the running backs are moving the ball down the field. It opens things up for you."

While Zabransky was satisfied with the team's overall performance, he remained hesi-

tant to be too content with his individual outing. Zabransky gave himself a "B" grading on his performance, feeling there is still room for improvement before Oregon State September 7.

"There were a lot of throws in there that I could have made, a couple decisions I would have changed, but I feel I played good. Like I said, that's easy to do when you got all day back there."

Coach Pete shared similar sentiments with Zabransky on his quarterback's opening-night performance.

"It was solid," Petersen said. "I know there were a couple things in there that he would like to do over. But, uh, we expect that guy to play perfect, that position to play perfect. I don't know if that's happened in the history of football, but we're going to keep trying. Trying to get that done. But I think he played well; played at a high level."

The BSU offense received a large load of support from the Bronco defense, which put overwhelming pressure on the Sacramento State offensive unit the entire night. The Hornets could only muster 82 totals yards from scrimmage for the game. Senior lineback Colt Brooks gave more than his share of big hits, including one ear-hole blast on a Quinton Jones punt return in the third, which sprung Jones for a 22-yard return up the sidelines. Brooks finished

	1st	2nd	3rd	4th	Final
Sacramento State	0	0	0	0	0
Boise State	21	7	10	7	45

Scoring Summary

1st

BSU: Johnson 19-yard run (Montgomery kick)—5 plays, 60 yards in 1:37.

BSU: Zabransky 1-yard run (Montgomery kick)—6 plays, 75 yards in 2:56.

BSU: Johnson 4-yard run (Montgomery kick)—2 plays, 16 yards in 0:28.

2nd

BSU: Naanee 3-yard pass from Zabransky (Montgomery kick)—5 plays, 34 yards in 2:38.

3rd

BSU: James 52-yard pass from Zabransky (Montgomery kick)—3 plays, 63 yards in 1:40.

BSU: Montgomery 33-yard field goal—6 plays, 22 yards in 2:22.

4th

BSU: Helmandollar 1-yard run (Montgomery kick)—14 plays, 71 yards in 7:06.

Team Statistics

	SAC	BSU
First Downs	3	22
Rushing Yards (Net)	50	215
Passing Yards (Net)	32	212
Passes (Comp-Att-Int)	6-15-2	15-24-0
Total Offense (Plays-Yards)	43-82	66-427
Fumble Returns-Yards	0-0	0-0
Punt Returns-Yards	2-11	6-70
Kickoff Returns-Yards	7-126	0-0
Interception-Yards	0-0	2-10
Punts (Number-Yards)	10-439	4-201
Fumbles-Lost	0-0	2-1
Sacks By (Number-Yards)	1-5	0-0
Penalties-Yards	11-86	4-26
Possession Time	28:42	31:18

with eight tackles and one interception in the game.

"[The game] was pretty good for the defense," Brooks said. "The last two weeks we've been really focused on playing a different team. It's hard playing against the same people in two-a-days, stuff like that. Coach Pete was really excited to release us. He knows how talented our defense is, returning nine starters. Coach Pete is always talking about focusing on ourselves and not the other team. I think we did that tonight."

As for the man in charge, Petersen was thrilled with getting his first victory out of the way and looks forward to carrying the momentum into Oregon State. His transition to the sidelines appeared to be a smooth one, but according to "Pete" there is much more to it than meets the eye.

"There's a little less to do on the sidelines than there is in the press box," Petersen said. "I'm more of a cheerleader. Hawk and I used to joke about that all the time. He had about 50 jokes about what he's actually doing on the sidelines. I was feeling his pain out there today."

While this game was the type of start Petersen and his staff were looking for to begin the year, the road will only get more difficult. While a win is always nice, there is no denying the Broncos will need all the momentum they can get to carry into a much more intense Oregon State game.

"There's a different animal coming to town next week," Petersen said. "This is the fourth year in a row we've played those guys (Oregon State). I was thinking about it the other day. I

was thinking 'Gosh, we used all our good plays on those guys; they've seen them all. We're gonna have to figure out some new ones.' But those guys are good. They (OSU) are a good program. They're a good team. It'll be a great challenge for us. But I know our kids will be looking forward to playing them."

The Boise State Broncos take the field prior to their game against Sacramento State. *Stanley Brewster/Arbiter*

WIDE RECEIVER JUMPS INTO SPOTLIGHT

BY JAKE GARCIN

Drisan James has seen enough of the good and bad times at Boise State to understand his role on this year's football team. Prior to the Bronco season opener against Sacramento State, however, everyone else had yet to figure out exactly what his role was going to be. After two 50-plus yard receptions, the picture is getting much clearer now.

One of the biggest question marks for Bronco fans during the off-season was who would step into the deep-threat role from the BSU receiving corps.

In recent years, Boise State quarterbacks have had the luxury of having at least one marquee wide receiver to provide quick-strike passing opportunities. Following a year in 2005 that gave no consistent downfield threat, Coach Petersen was looking for someone to step into that role this year. After game one of the '06 season, it appears he may have found his guy.

James burned the Hornet secondary twice August 31; once on a 56-yard play that led to a Bronco touchdown, and once on a 52-yard touchdown pass from Jared Zabransky on the first BSU drive of the second half. James finished with only three receptions for the game, but totaled 125 yards and one touchdown. James recognized after the game that he's just doing his job to help his team win.

Drisan James leaps in the air to complete a play against Sacramento State.
Stanley Brewster/Arbiter

"It gets the whole team started off like that," James said. "I mean, all the receivers actually see one receiver getting a 100-yard game, you know that's a motivation factor for them to get another 100-yard game. It's gonna be an all-around performance, it's gonna push everybody. I was fortunate to have guys to help me out.

"I'm fortunate to have a good receiver inside, as well as a bunch of backups that are also good to run the inside route and bring the safety down to give me a one-on-one match-up," James said.

The Sacramento State game proved to be a valuable learning experience for the entire team and staff.

Although no one claims they have been looking ahead to their match-up with Oregon State on September 7, James admits their first win is a step in the right direction to preparing for the Beavers.

"Obviously last year things didn't turn out too good in Georgia," James said. "It kind of put us down a little bit. This year, we know that things are gonna happen, that not everything is gonna

Drisan James runs the ball past teammates in Boise State's annual Blue and Orange Scrimmage.
Stanley Brewster/Arbiter

team went down into the slumps. This year we've just got to take things a game at a time."

While James appears to be willing to step into the spotlight this season, he also seems to be staying grounded. James accepts the credit, but isn't losing sight of the Bronco team concept.

"The (offensive) line, hands down, was the best performance by far. If it wasn't for the line, I wouldn't be sitting here right now getting the post game interview."

As far accolades are concerned, for James, the warm reception by the BSU fans is all the reward he needs. The Boise State faithful prides itself in being one of the best home crowds in the country; according to James, that's not far from the truth.

> "THIS YEAR WE'VE JUST GOT TO TAKE THINGS A GAME AT A TIME."
>
> BSU WIDE RECEIVER DRISAN JAMES

"We love the crowd," James said.

"Whenever we hear that Boise State chant that gets everybody fired up, it gets the hairs on the back just sticking straight up. We love the fans. I wish that every time we score we could interact with the fans, but you know the refs are gonna throw a big hissy fit about it."

James' next challenge comes against a much more experienced OSU secondary, in a game that should give the entire BSU offense a chance to show their early season success isn't a fluke.

be pretty. Even though we did beat them (Sacramento State) by 45, we also feel we got to take it a game at a time. That's what we didn't do last year; instead we took the season as a whole. Since we lost the first game our whole

23

ZABRANSKY TAKES CENTER STAGE

BY JAKE GARCIN

Every football season acts as a farewell tour for another Boise State senior class. While every game is important, there are always one or two games on a schedule that stand out as the one players want to play their best in.

For senior quarterback Jared Zabransky, one last game against Oregon State is one last chance to make sure the Beavers realize what they could have had if they'd taken a chance on him four years ago.

Zabransky grew up playing football in a small Northeast Oregon town, looking at Oregon State as one of the programs he would one day like to be a part of. Despite a great high school career at Hermiston High School, neither the University of Oregon nor Oregon State showed much interest in the budding star.

Faced with limited options, Zabransky picked Boise State and has never looked back on his way to a record-book career at BSU.

"It basically came down to here and (University of) Idaho because they were my only two offers," Zabransky said.

"They (Oregon State) and Oregon both recruited me, but it wasn't anything special. Oregon State asked me to walk on real late, but there was no chance of that. I'm glad I came here, and I wouldn't change it for anything else."

This year's meeting with OSU will be the third time Zabransky has faced the Beavers as a starter. In the previous two games, Jared has done his fair share of damage to the Oregon State defense.

Jared Zabransky prepares to throw a pass during a preseason practice.
Stanley Brewster/Arbiter

In 2004 Zabransky completed 20 of 34 passes for 225 yards with three touchdowns. Jared also rushed for 73 yards and a touchdown in route to a 53-34 win.

Last year Zabransky's performance was almost identical, throwing for 233 yards and three touchdowns with 19 completions on 36 attempts in the 30-27 Bronco loss.

With one final showdown coming on September 7, Zabransky is hopeful that his final game against OSU will be his best. A task, however, that won't be easy to complete.

"I feel a little extra motivated to get after these guys," Zabransky said. "Everybody that comes to Boise State was slightly overlooked or they're from a small school that didn't get any looks. All of us feel like we're big-time players, so it's kind of a 'chip on the shoulder' mentality."

In his two seasons leading the Bronco offense with a chip on his shoulder, Zabransky has found his way into the top five in the BSU record books for total offensive yards during a season and a career, as well as top five for single-season passing yards and career passing yards.

Jared also landed in the top five for single-season completions in both 2004 and 2005. Needless to say, Zabransky has proved his worth to everyone who overlooked him in high school, including of course, Oregon State.

"THIS HAS BEEN A GREAT PIECE OF MY HISTORY. TO PLAY AN OREGON SCHOOL, AND TO PLAY THEM AS TOUGH AS WE HAVE. IT'S SOMETHING THAT I WILL TREASURE FOREVER."

BSU QUARTERBACK
JARED ZABRANSKY

As for the rest of the team, Oregon State will give the Broncos a perfect opportunity to evaluate their progress from the end of last year. Having a game against a team from a major conference year in and year out gives BSU a chance to gauge their progress on a national level. A win against a program like Oregon State will also bring increased credibility to the Western Athletic Conference, helping Boise State's push to a Bowl Championship Series bowl game.

"You know we need to take advantage of the opportunities," Zabransky said. "The WAC had a pretty good showing last week, even though we didn't win very many games. That's something we have to do to help this conference out and gain a little more respect. But you know, we're focused on what we have to do, we have to play well against Oregon State. If those other teams win, that's good for them, but we're really focused on Oregon State."

The game against OSU will be the fourth meeting between the two teams in as many seasons. Despite the recent growth in the rivalry, however, OSU isn't on Boise State's schedule for any seasons in the near future.

The absence of the Beavers could end up leaving a void in the Bronco schedule for years to come.

Jared Zabransky runs the ball during the Broncos' first regular-season game in 2006.
Stanley Brewster/Arbiter

"We feel like we match up very well with these guys," Zabransky said. "Every time we have the opportunity to play a Pac-10 team, especially getting them at home two years out of the four is a great opportunity for us.

"I think it's become a rivalry," Zabransky said. "Any time you have two pretty evenly matched teams that come out and want to win the football game and want to play hard; it turns into good football games, exciting football games. I think that kind of builds a rivalry. I would be excited to see them try and keep it on the schedule."

So with all the story lines surrounding this year's game and the game being the last between these two great football programs for at least a couple years; it is only fitting that the Oregon grown boy will be leading Boise State down the field Thursday night.

"This has been a great piece of my history," Zabransky said. "To play an Oregon school, and to play them as tough as we have. It's something that I will treasure forever."

JOHNSON SKINS BEAVERS' DEFENSE ON RECORD NIGHT

BY JAKE GARCIN

Bronco Stadium grew deathly silent September 7 after Oregon State scored their second touchdown in a two-minute span during the opening quarter against Boise State. The 14-point cushion wouldn't be nearly enough as the Broncos rolled out 42 unanswered points to turn a bad start into a blow out. For the third consecutive year, the BSU and OSU match-up ended with the team on the board 14-0 going on to lose the game.

Boise State's 42-14 spanking of the Beavers gave way to a record-setting night for one Bronco that is quickly becoming a household name in Boise.

Running back Ian Johnson cut loose for 138 yards rushing on 13 carries and three touchdowns; and then the horn blew to end the second quarter. After half-time Johnson continued his terror, tallying 240 yards on the ground on just 22 carries and tied a team-record five touchdowns. Johnson broke a 59-yard run to put the first Bronco points on the scoreboard. He also broke a run up the gut in the fourth quarter for a 50-yard scamper to the end zone.

Behind an ever-so-impressive offensive line,

Johnson seemed to answer any questions that still lingered about his ability to be a feature back in the Boise State offense.

"You know I try not to think about that type of stuff," Johnson said. "I'm the type of person that I just forget about it until the game starts. You know, whatever they throw at me, I conditioned myself so hard during the summer that I know no matter what they throw at us they conditioned us for it. I just trust the system so much that they got me ready for 35 carries if I take 35 carries. So whether I was ready or not, in my mind I was ready."

Senior quarterback Jared Zabransky was one of the Bronco players who appeared to take a back seat to Johnson's historic night. Despite filling the pre-game conversation going up against OSU one last time, Zabransky put up less than eye-popping numbers against the Beavers. While only throwing the ball 13 times, Zabransky completed eight passes for 105 yards. Contrary to what the statistics read, Coach Petersen was pleased with his quarterback's performance, and stated it was exactly what the team needed to succeed.

Jeff Cavender (64) hoists Ian Johnson (41) up after Johnson's fifth and final touchdown against the Beavers.

Stanley Brewster/Arbiter

Broncos head coach Chris Petersen motions from the sideline. *Stanley Brewster/Arbiter*

"I thought he played really well," Petersen said. "His stats aren't gonna show that. We keep talking about him being efficient and not having to win the game. But he was doing a lot of things out there. He manages the game very well for us. He has no turnovers. This time last year was a different story. You know, he's definitely taken the step we need him to take."

The Boise State defense settled down following the two early OSU scores and played a shut out for the last 51 minutes of the game. Senior linebacker Korey Hall led the team in tackles with 10, giving a performance worthy of all the national recognition he received during pre-season workouts.

"Obviously, tonight we weren't happy with that first drive," Hall said. "You know, we kind of changed some stuff up with our front and the D-line started firing off and I think that helped."

Hall also caught the only interception of the game, which led to the second Bronco touchdown and tied the game at 14 apiece.

"I think whenever we get a turnover on defense it's good for us," Hall said. "You know that's kind of what we thrive on and I think it helps our offense also.

"I'm always trying to get interceptions, not that it always happens," Hall said. "I think that play they ran, they had run a few plays before that but we went off-sides so they didn't get to run it all the way out. I kind of noticed it and kind of broke out of my area and made the play."

The Boise State defense was also able to bounce back after the first defensive series and contain Oregon State's rushing attack behind Yvenson Bernard. Bernard rushed for 150 yards in the Beavers' opener at Eastern Washington University and appeared to be on track again against the Broncos, gaining 50 yards on the

Korey Hall intercepts a pass in the second quarter.
Stanley Brewster/Arbiter

30

	1st	2nd	3rd	4th	Final
Oregon State	14	0	0	0	14
Boise State	7	21	7	7	42

Scoring Summary

1st

OSU: Newton 3-yard pass from Moore (Serna kick)—12 plays, 85 yards in 6:44.

OSU: Stroughter 64-yard punt return (Serna kick).

BSU: Johnson 59-yard run (Montgomery kick)—4 plays, 71 yards in 2:10.

2nd

BSU: Johnson 4-yard run (Montgomery kick)—5 plays, 41 yards in 2:02.

BSU: Johnson 3-yard run (Montgomery kick)—9 plays, 80 yards in 4:06.

BSU: Naanee 3-yard pass from Zabransky (Montgomery kick)—6 plays, 60 yards in 2:40.

3rd

BSU: Johnson 19-yard run (Montgomery kick)—1 play, 19 yards in 0:20.

4th

BSU: Johnson 50-yard run (Montgomery kick)—1 play, 50 yards in 0:21.

Team Statistics

	OSU	BSU
First Downs	14	19
Rushing Yards (Net)	58	302
Passing Yards (Net)	205	105
Passes (Comp-Att-Int)	20-29-1	8-14-0
Total Offense (Plays-Yards)	61-263	56-407
Fumble Returns-Yards	0-0	0-0
Punt Returns-Yards	3-74	2-17
Kickoff Returns-Yards	4-93	1-22
Interceptions-Yards	0-0	1-3
Punts (Number-Yards)	5-185	5-231
Fumbles-Lost	2-2	1-1
Sacks By (Number-Yards)	3-22	6-31
Penalties-Yards	7-73	7-50
Possession Time	33:41	26:19

first OSU offensive drive. However, after tightening up the BSU front line, Bernard was only able to scrape 39 more yards over the next three and a half quarters.

"The kids did a great job rallying back," Coach Petersen said. "They really did. They didn't flinch. They didn't blink. They just kept playing, charging forward."

Boise State travels to the University of Wyoming next, where the Broncos will look to continue their campaign toward a Bowl Championship Series bid at season's end. Coach Petersen will look to keep his team grounded and hungry for the Wyoming Cowboys to avoid an unpleasant trip home from Laramie.

"I think that our guys know what they need to do, and they're going to stay grounded," Petersen said. "Some of the things we went through last year, they have learned that they have to show up and practice hard on Tuesday, Wednesday, and Thursday for us to keep improving.

"If we would have lost that game (Oregon State), my mentality going out to practice would be no different. I may have been more in the tank, and been a little more ticked off. But in terms of what we've got to get done to keep taking a step forward: no different."

Running back Ian Johnson scores one of his five touchdowns against Oregon State.
Stalney Brewster/Arbiter

BRONCOS BUCK COWBOYS

BY JAKE GARCIN

It was a battle between "cowboy tough" and "blue collar" work ethic in Laramie, Wyoming, when the Boise State football team traveled to the University of Wyoming for the Broncos' first road game of the season. The Broncos managed to hold off a late Cowboy push for a 17-10 win to improve their season record to 3-0.

A tough UW defense wasn't the only opponent Coach Petersen's guys had to fight with on September 16. The game was surrounded by 35 miles per hour winds, which made the BSU offense reliant on their running attack once again. The game-time temperature was a brisk 46 degrees, but with a 37-degree wind chill and a short snow flurry filling the stadium, Petersen and company were tested against the cold for the first time all year.

After building a 17-point lead in the first half, BSU needed a late interception by Orlando Scandrick to stop the Cowboys' final push to tie the score with just 2:20 left in regulation.

Drisan James attempts to haul in a pass for the Broncos.
Stanley Brewster/Arbiter

"We got a lot of confidence in our defense," Bronco quarterback Jared Zabransky said. "We knew we needed to get the ball back, we knew what we had to do, and we went and did it."

Scandrick's interception came after a one-yard quarterback keeper by Jacob Doss with 8:02 left to play in the fourth quarter. The score was followed by a UW defensive stand that held the Broncos to three and out on their next offensive possession. Despite having momentum on the Wyoming sidelines for the first time all afternoon, Doss was picked off for the second time in the game, ending the Cowboys' hope of a last-second upset.

Wyoming did find the scoreboard first with a 31-yard field goal from Aric Goodman on the first drive of the game. Boise State answered with a field goal of its own from Anthony Montgomery to even the score at three after the first period. The Broncos received their only offensive touchdown of the game on a six-yard run by Zabransky, capping a 13-play, 84-yard drive.

Quinton Jones returned an interception 61 yards for a score midway through the second quarter. The touchdown wound up being the deciding score of the contest.

Quinton Jones (23) and Orlando Scandrick (8) attempt to catch the incoming pass.

Stanley Brewster/Arbiter

"WE KNEW WE NEEDED TO GET THE BALL BACK, WE KNEW WHAT WE HAD TO DO, AND WE WENT AND DID IT."

BSU QUARTERBACK
JARED ZABRANSKY

Boise State head coach Chris Petersen recognized the defensive effort after the game, but he also admitted the offensive will have some adjustments to make after a less-than-spectacular performance.

"We're going to go over the tape with a fine-tooth comb," Petersen said. "There were some mistakes. The weather had some to do with it, but we have things we need to correct.

"This was a good game for our team," Petersen said. "Our defense was spectacular and I will say this; our offense didn't turn the ball over, which was big. If we continue to play good defense and not turn the ball over, we're gonna continue to win some games."

Despite tallying only 246 offensive yards against the Cowboy defense, it was the Bronco ability to keep hold of the football that proved to be the difference maker in the game. Running back Ian Johnson provided his second consecutive 100-yard rushing performance of the season, finishing with 119 yards on 23 carries. Zabransky was barely over the century mark in passing for the second consecutive game, completing 12 of 20 passes for 116 yards. However, once again the Broncos found a balanced offensive attack to give their defense just enough cushion to stay perfect on the season.

On defense it was senior linebacker Korey Hall who led the BSU defense once again. Hall led the team in tackles with 11. Six of Hall's tackles were assisted. Hall also recorded his

	1st	2nd	3rd	4th	Final
Boise State	**3**	**14**	**0**	**0**	**17**
Wyoming	**3**	**0**	**0**	**7**	**10**

Scoring Summary

1st

WY: Goodman 31-yard field goal—13 plays, 67 yards in 5:15.

BSU: Montgomery 23-yard field goal—12 plays, 56 yards in 6:29.

2nd

BSU: Zabransky 6-yard run (Montgomery kick)—13 plays, 84 yards in 5:37.

BSU: Jones 61-yard interception return (Montgomery kick).

WY: Doss 1-yard run (Goodman kick)—12 plays, 55 yards in 6:12.

Team Statistics

	BSU	WY
First Downs	17	15
Rushing Yards (Net)	130	73
Passing Yards (Net)	116	178
Passes (Comp-Att-Int)	12-21-0	14-30-2
Total Offense (Plays-Yards)	62-246	59-251
Fumble Returns-Yards	0-0	0-0
Punt Returns-Yards	3-14	1-13
Kickoff Returns-Yards	3-72	2-38
Interceptions-Yards	2-86	0-0
Punts (Number-Yards)	7-351	6-269
Fumbles-Lost	1-0	0-0
Sacks By (Number-Yards)	5-18	3-23
Penalties-Yards	7-55	8-45
Possession Time	30:08	29:52

first sack of the season. He finished with one and a half sacks officially in the game.

Boise State returns home for its first Western Athletic Conference game of the season when Hawaii visits Boise Saturday, September 23. With a win against Wyoming, BSU remains in contention for a Bowl Championship Series bid at season's end. However, there are far more important things on the minds of the Bronco players with 75 percent of the season still ahead.

"We're not thinking about an undefeated season," Orlando Scandrick said after the Wyoming game. "We are gonna take it a game at a time. We know championship teams have to win some dog fights, but we aren't thinking too far ahead."

"WE'RE NOT THINKING ABOUT AN UNDEFEATED SEASON. WE ARE GONNA TAKE IT A GAME AT A TIME."

BSU CORNERBACK
ORLANDO SCANDRICK

Tad Miller waits for the ball to be snapped at the line of scrimmage. *Stanley Brewster/Arbiter*

PETERSEN LEADS BRONCOS BACK TO TOP 25

BY JAKE GARCIN

"Earn national respect." This motivating goal has become a common theme for the Boise State football program since head coach Chris Petersen took over as offensive coordinator in 2001.

On Sunday, September 16, Coach Petersen's Broncos garnered that national respect, finding their way into the Associated Press and College Coaches top 25 polls for the fifth consecutive season.

Although 2006 is Petersen's first year in charge of the program, it is clear that the team's progress toward becoming a national power hasn't skipped a beat. After a 3-0 start to the year, Boise State has gotten one monkey off its back, but now faces new challenges to prove it deserves to be in the spotlight.

"I think the bull's-eye is always big now here at Boise State," Petersen said. "I think everyone kind of knows what they're gonna get; we're gonna fight them hard, play hard, and play them tough.

"So (the bull's-eye) probably grows a little bit, but I don't know if it's that much more than what people think about coming here to play us on the blue turf anyways."

One of the ultimate goals that remains elusive to Boise State football is a bid to a Bowl Championship Series game in January. One of the new changes to the BCS selection process is an at-large bid by a non-BCS conference team.

With the addition of an extra BCS bowl game, there will be room for one mid-major team, assuming that team finishes higher in the polls than one of the BCS conference champions.

Boise State will have to leap frog Texas Christian University by season's end, as TCU currently sits at number 15 in both polls and would receive the at-large bid if the opportunity came about.

Currently, the BCS is comprised of the Pacific 10, Big 12, Big 10, Big East and Atlantic Coast

Chris Petersen watches his team from the Boise State sidelines.
Stanley Brewster/Arbiter

conferences. Each of these five conferences receives an automatic BCS bid for the champion of their respective conference.

So with plenty of stipulations left to be played out over the next two months, all Coach Petersen can do is take the season one game at a time. A crucial focus for the Broncos as a very dangerous University of Hawaii team visits Boise September 23.

"Everyone always thinks you have to stop the pass (with Hawaii)," Petersen said. "Which you do, but first and foremost you have to stop the run. We've done very well in the past stopping the run game, and I think you have to make sure it's totally one-dimensional to have a chance."

Hawaii came into the 2006 season with little expectations from the rest of the country. The Warriors were voted the No. 4 team in the Western Athletic Conference Preseason Coaches' Poll.

However, with two former NFL coaches running the program and top-level quarterback Colt Brennan, Hawaii comes to Boise as one of the scariest teams BSU has to face this season.

"I wish I was playing against a couple guys that don't know football," Petersen said. "That would crank me up. (Brennan) is one of those guys who has a good feel for the game. His instincts are very good. For me, that's one of those commodities that you can't estimate."

The match-up against Hawaii will be the first WAC game of the season for BSU.

With five consecutive conference championships on the line and the task of proving they deserve a top-25 ranking, the pressure to succeed is apparent for the Broncos.

"I think the competition level that we're starting to play is getting tougher and tougher, but I don't think that distracts us. I mean, we've got guys that are fairly mature, and it's something we talked about way back in the summer time. Not getting caught up in rankings. Our record right now is 0-0. It really wouldn't matter what our true record is. We just have to go out each week and play the best we can."

During a home game against Louisiana Tech, Chris Petersen tries to gain the attention of his players.
Stanley Brewster/Arbiter

BOISE STATE SURVIVES SHOOTOUT

BY JAKE GARCIN

Boise State recorded its first Western Athletic Conference win on September 23 with a 41-34 victory against the high-powered run-and-shoot offense of the University of Hawaii. The Broncos opened a game with a 15-point lead, but the rest of the night was full of twists and turns.

The Bronco offense first found the end zone two and a half minutes into the first quarter on a three-yard Ian Johnson touchdown run. After forcing a three and out on the first Warrior offensive possession, it only took three plays for the Broncos to march 57 yards and score. Quarterback Jared Zabransky found Jerard Rabb for a 24-yard completion on the first play from scrimmage for Boise State. After a 24-yard scamper by Johnson on the second offensive play of the game, he punched it in from three yards out to take a 7-0 lead.

Jared Zabransky hands off to Ian Johnson during their game against Hawaii.
Stanley Brewster/Arbiter

BSU capitalized next when Hawaii receiver Devone Bess fumbled the ball after a 44-yard catch and run, which was forced by Gerald Alexander and recovered by the Broncos. From there, it took seven plays for BSU to extend its lead to 15-0. Zabransky found Legedu Naanee on a seven-yard pass that Bronco offensive coordinator Bryan Harsin capped off with a fake PAT attempt. The successful two-point conversion gave BSU a 15-point lead at the end of the first quarter.

Hawaii gave its first answer to BSU's quick offensive strike with an 11-yard touchdown pass from standout quarterback Colt Brennan. The score was the first of five touchdown passes by Brennan for the game. However, Boise State was able to counter with a 23-yard touchdown pass to tight end Derek Schouman and a defensive PAT return by Orlando Scandrick after Hawaii's second botched snap on a point after try. Anthony Montgomery finished the first-half scoring with a 32-yard field goal with 13 seconds left in the first half, giving BSU a 24-14 half-time lead.

The intermission didn't slow down either offense, as BSU marched 65 yards down the field on the first offensive drive of the third quarter. Ian Johnson found the end zone for the sec-

Running back Brett Denton picks up positive yardage against the Hawaii defense.
Stanley Brewster/Arbiter

ond time in the game on an eight-yard run just three and a half minutes into the half. Hawaii managed to keep the game close with a 14-yard touchdown pass to Devone Bess.

Hawaii continued to put pressure on the BSU defense throughout the fourth quarter, scoring twice on passes from Brennan. However, a second touchdown catch by Schouman with just less than six minutes left in the game put the Broncos out of reach once and for all. Boise State ran the clock out on a fourth-down conversion with just over a minute left to play. Ian Johnson broke the Warrior defense one last time on a fourth and one that Johnson broke for 16 yards to finish off the Hawaii rally.

Johnson totaled 178 rushing yards for the game on 29 carries with two rushing touchdowns. It was the third consecutive game Johnson managed to break 100 yards rushing.

Senior quarterback Jared Zabransky threw his first interception of the season, yet still compiled his best outing of the year with a 17-for-29 passing performance for 273 yards. Zabransky's interception came on a third-and-goal play from the 27-yard line.

"I thought (Jared) threw the ball very well in practice all week and it really carried over to the game," Boise State head coach Chris Petersen said.

"I know everybody wants (Zabransky) to throw 40 passes a game and I know he wants to

	1st	2nd	3rd	4th	Final
Hawaii	0	14	7	13	34
Boise State	15	12	7	7	41

Scoring Summary

1st

BSU: Johnson 3-yard run (Montgomery kick)–3 plays, 43 yards in 0:33.

BSU: Naanee 6-yard pass from Zabransky (Stringer rush)–6 plays, 57 yards in 2:41.

2nd

HAW: Rivers 26-yard pass from Brennan (Milne rush fumbled)–5 plays, 76 yards in 2:23.

BSU: Scandrick PAT return.

BSU: Schouman 23-yard pass from Zabransky (Montgomery kick)–4 plays, 86 yards in 2:13.

HAW: Rivers 11-yard pass from Brennan (Bess pass from Brennan)–5 plays, 73 yards in 2:17.

BSU: Montgomery 32-yard field goal–13 plays, 64 yards in 3:04.

3rd

BSU: Johnson 8-yard run (Montgomery kick)–8 plays, 65 yards in 3:18.

HAW: Bess 18-yard pass from Brennan (Kelly kick)–4 plays, 57 yards in 1:48.

4th

HAW: Bess 14-yard pass from Brennan (Kelly pass failed)–11 plays, 81 yards in 3:42.

BSU: Schouman 18-yard pass from Zabransky (Montgomery kick)–8 plays, 55 yards in 4:22.

HAW: Rivers 8-yard pass from Brennan (Kelly kick)–8 plays, 64 yards in 2:56.

Team Statistics

	HAW	BSU
First Downs	24	26
Rushing Yards (Net)	88	242
Passing Yards (Net)	388	273
Passes (Comp-Att-Int)	25-37-1	17-29-1
Total Offense (Plays-Yards)	55-476	73-515
Fumble Returns-Yards	0-0	0-0
Punt Returns-Yards	2-27	1-16
Kickoff Returns-Yards	4-84	3-60
Interceptions-Yards	1-19	1-16
Punts (Number-Yards)	2-83	4-180
Fumbles-Lost	2-2	1-0
Sacks By (Number-Yards)	1-9	2-4
Penalties-Yards	4-23	9-90
Possession Time	24:58	35:02

throw 40 passes, but that kid's a winner and he's doing a great job. He's doing whatever we ask him to do to win the game. If that means running the ball 50 times a game, he'll do that and you know there will be games where we're more balanced, we like to be balanced, and I think we were very balanced tonight. And that's where we think we're most effective and probably most dangerous."

As far as slowing down the high-powered Hawaii offense, the Bronco defense refused to get discouraged by its inability to shut down the wide-open Warrior passing attack.

"We knew if we didn't just put them away early that they're the type of team that they don't care if they throw an interception, they don't care," BSU running back Ian Johnson said. "They'll just keep going. They keep hitting big plays, it might only take one play. They'll throw it deep on first down and 15, they'll try and get a home run every time so we knew we had to keep putting up points and give our defense something to work with. And we were doing fine with it. We have a high-powered offense and we wanted to show what we can do."

Senior linebacker Colt Brooks played a less-than-typical game for Boise State, only recording two tackles for the night. However, being played up on the defensive line all game long influenced most of Brooks' defensive production. Korey Hall led the team in tackles once again, with 13 total and five unassisted.

"It's difficult. The defense didn't play as well as, you know, we planned on," Brooks said. "But you know the offense stuck through for us. We

Garrett Tuggle carries the sledgehammer and leads the charge onto the field before the Broncos' game against Hawaii.
Stanley Brewster/Arbiter

just struggled with certain plays and we were trying to figure them out and they kept us thinking and it was a tough game for the defense. But it's a good thing the offense was there to stick it through and help us out."

Boise State travels to the University of Utah September 30 for the Broncos' last non-conference game of the season. The win over Hawaii may prove to be a crucial one, as many people recognize Hawaii as the biggest threat to a fifth-consecutive WAC championship for Boise State.

"Well, it was just a little bit different than I thought it was going to go," Coach Petersen said.

"You know we always have interesting games with Hawaii. They're usually kind of high scoring, but I thought it would be more of a defensive struggle. I thought teams would get points on big plays, but it seemed like both offenses were just kind of marching down the field and nobody could stop each other. And I just didn't predict it going like that."

BOISE STATE BOUNCES UTAH 36-3

BY JAKE GARCIN

Most of Rice-Eccles Stadium cleared at the end of the third quarter in the game between Boise State and Utah. The Broncos were up 33-3 and had field position at Utah's 40-yard line after the fourth interception of the game by the BSU defense. As the clock ran out, nearly 4,000 Bronco fans remained, chanting a clear message to the world: BCS!

Following Texas Christian University's upset loss on September 28, the Broncos were lifted into the most likely spot for a Bowl Championship Series bid. It took a quarter to heat up the Boise State engine, but for the last 45 minutes of the game the Broncos sent the message that they are up to any challenge.

"WE FELT IT, WE FELT THE ELECTRICITY. THERE WAS DEFINITELY A DIFFERENT AURA THAN OTHER GAMES."

BSU QUARTERBACK JARED ZABRANSKY

Boise State linebacker Korey Hall created the first scoring opportunity of the game just four plays into Utah's first offensive series. Hall grabbed his first of two interceptions and returned the ball to the Utah 21-yard line. Boise State scored its only points of the first quarter four plays later on a 35-yard field goal kick by Anthony Montgomery.

Kyle Gingg sacks Utah quarterback Brett Ratliff.
Stanley Brewster/Arbiter

The Bronco defense forced a punt on the next Utah offensive possession, starting the second Bronco offensive drive on the one-yard line. The poor field position didn't last long, however, as Jared Zabransky found Jerard Rabb for a 39-yard completion and what looked like a rally-inducing catch. Rabb tipped the pass to himself in close coverage and came down with the ball, falling onto his back.

Utah countered quickly, swinging the momentum back momentarily as safety Eric Weddle stepped in front and intercepted Zabransky at the 50-yard line. The Utes managed a drive to the Boise State 20-yard line before converting a 37-yard Louie Sakoda field goal to tie the score 3-3.

The second quarter proved to be more explosive for the Bronco offense and opportunistic for the defense. BSU started the second quarter with a third-and-one on the Utah six-yard line. Despite a false start penalty that pushed the Broncos back to a third and long, Zabransky found Brett Denton for an eight-yard completion and the first down. One play later Zabransky connected with fullback Brad Lau for a three-yard touchdown pass and a 10-3 Bronco lead.

The Bronco defense forced another short offensive series for the Utes. After a short six-play drive, BSU regained possession with another Utah punt. The Bronco offense was able to put together a nine-play, 59-yard drive before running back Ian Johnson fumbled the ball at the Utah four-yard line. Johnson broke two tackles on the 14-yard run before defensive back Steve Tate forced the ball out of Johnson's arms.

The Boise State defense held strong once again, however, forcing yet another Utah punt from the eight-yard line. Zabransky led the offense down inside the Utah 20 with a completion to tight end Derek Schouman. The Broncos ran a double pass play, in which the ball was touched by running back Vinny Perretta, Zabransky and finally by Schouman. Zabransky suffered a cut on his right wrist after smacking his hand against the helmet of a Utah defender on the play. Zabransky returned on the next drive of the game, but did say afterward that he would be needing stitches.

Boise State fullback Brad Lau makes an extra effort as he is brought down by a Utah player. *Stanley Brewster/Arbiter*

Backup quarterback Taylor Tharp was needed for just one play as Perretta found the end zone on the next play from scrimmage. The eight-yard sweep to the left side of the field pushed the score to 16-3, despite a missed point attempt by Montgomery.

The Utes never recovered from the Boise State scoring run, as quarterback Brett Ratliff was intercepted for a second time just three plays into the next Utah drive. Senior linebacker Colt Brooks intercepted Ratliff at the 12-yard line and returned it untouched for another Bronco touchdown and a 23-3 half-time lead.

The Bronco offense appeared not to lose any momentum at the break as Montgomery kicked a 40-yard field goal through the uprights, concluding a nine-play drive to begin the second half. Korey Hall intercepted his second pass of the game, this time off of backup quarterback Tommy Grady. Grady replaced Ratliff to start the second half but was unable to produce for the Utes. Hall returned the interception 43 yards

	1st	2nd	3rd	4th	Final
Boise State	3	20	10	3	36
Utah	3	0	0	0	3

Scoring Summary

1st

BSU: Montgomery 35-yard field goal—4 plays, 3 yards in 1:51.

UU: Sakoda 37-yard field goal—5 plays, 30 yards in 1:20.

2nd

BSU: Lau 3-yard pass from Zabransky (Montgomery kick)—11 plays, 80 yards in 6:19.

BSU: Perretta 8-yard run (Montgomery kick failed)—4 plays, 57 yards in 1:24.

BSU: Brooks 12-yard interception return (Montgomery kick)

3rd

BSU: Montgomery 40-yard field goal—10 plays, 57 yards in 5:11.

BSU: Zabransky 1-yard run (Montgomery kick)—3 plays, 2 yards in 1:38.

4th

BSU: Montgomery 22-yard field goal—10 plays, 36 yards in 4:32.

Team Statistics

	BSU	UU
First Downs	18	8
Rushes-Yards (Net)	188	127
Passing Yards (Net)	210	51
Passes (Comp-Att-Int)	15-22-2	8-27-4
Total Offense (Plays-Yards)	64-398	56-178
Fumble Returns-Yards	0-0	0-0
Punt Returns-Yards	2-6	1-9
Kickoff Returns-Yards	0-0	3-62
Interception-Yards	4-73	2-6
Punts (Number-Yards)	2-79	7-314
Fumbles-Lost	2-1	1-0
Sacks By (Number-Yards)	0-0	1-10
Penalties-Yards	5-35	5-34
Possession Time	32:20	27:40

before putting the ball on the ground with an attempted lateral to Kyle Gingg. Gingg managed to fall on the ball at the Utah two-yard line. BSU punched in their fourth touchdown of the day on a Zabransky one-yard keeper three plays later.

Following the last Ratliff interception, most of the 45,222 fans in attendance left having seen enough and giving the Boise State cheering section virtual control of the stadium for the final quarter.

"We came out for warm ups and our fans were louder than their fans booing us," Zabransky said. "We felt it, we felt the electricity. There was definitely a different aura than other games."

The Bronco defense held Ratliff and Grady to just 51 passing yards for the game with four interceptions. All four Bronco interceptions led to points for Boise State. Hall led the Bronco defense with his two picks and a team-high eight tackles.

"I think, again, it came down to when you get that many turnovers because of awesome pass coverage you get pressure on the QB," Bronco head coach Chris Petersen said. "When we get it rolling on both sides they start to feed off each other."

Offensively, the Bronco attack was powered by a very balanced running game. Ian Johnson finished with 89 yards on just 14 carries. Meanwhile, backup Vinny Perretta provided the biggest offensive lift with a 69-yard performance on 12 carries with one touchdown. Perretta's performance was by far his best of the year for the Broncos.

54

Legedu Naanee reaches for a catch in front of Utah's Eric Weddle. *Stanley Brewster/Arbiter*

"We've got a lot of respect for Utah," Petersen said. "You could see it in the kids how hard they played. We stepped up to the challenge and I think they feel good about themselves."

With the win Boise State improves their record to 5-0 and are steadily moving up in the nation's top 25 rankings. The game was also the last preseason game of the year for BSU. The victory at Utah improves Boise State's record to 11-0 against Mountain West Conference opponents.

"It says a lot about our program and where it has come from," Zabransky said. "I think the WAC and the Mountain West have about the same level of talent that they get. Boise State is continuing to prove points and continuing to up the standards."

BOISE STATE POUNDS BULLDOGS

BY JAKE GARCIN

The Boise State football team posted a 55-14 blowout over Louisiana Tech October 7 at Bronco Stadium. The win came despite an early scare from the Bulldogs.

LA Tech struck so quickly BSU found itself down 7-0 just 1:05 into the first quarter. Bronco kick returner Quinton Jones fumbled the opening kick off, which was recovered by LA Tech at the Boise State 14-yard line. The Bulldog offense found the end zone four plays later on a one-yard run by Patrick Jackson.

"I don't know that it woke us up," BSU head coach Chris Petersen said. "The games never go like you think they're gonna. There's always some phase that happens certainly different than we predicted. I think in the long run when you come out ahead they're good for us."

The quick Bulldog strike proved to be the only one for the next 58 minutes of the game.

Following the Jackson touchdown, Boise State's defense wouldn't allow another point until 0:34 to go in the fourth quarter. Meanwhile, the Bronco offense rallied off 31 unanswered points to garner a 31-7 halftime lead.

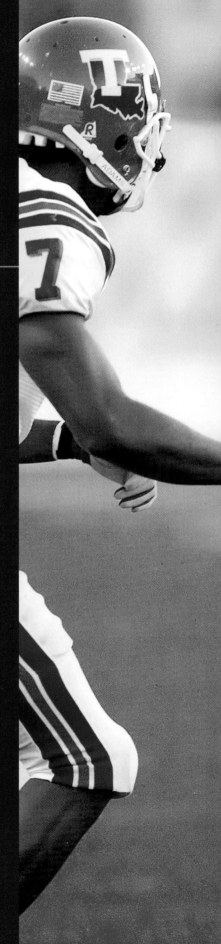

Marty Tadman (20) and the Broncos defense swarm the Louisiana Tech ball carrier.
Stanley Brewster/Arbiter

OCTOBER 7, 2006 • BRONCOS 55, BULLDOGS 14

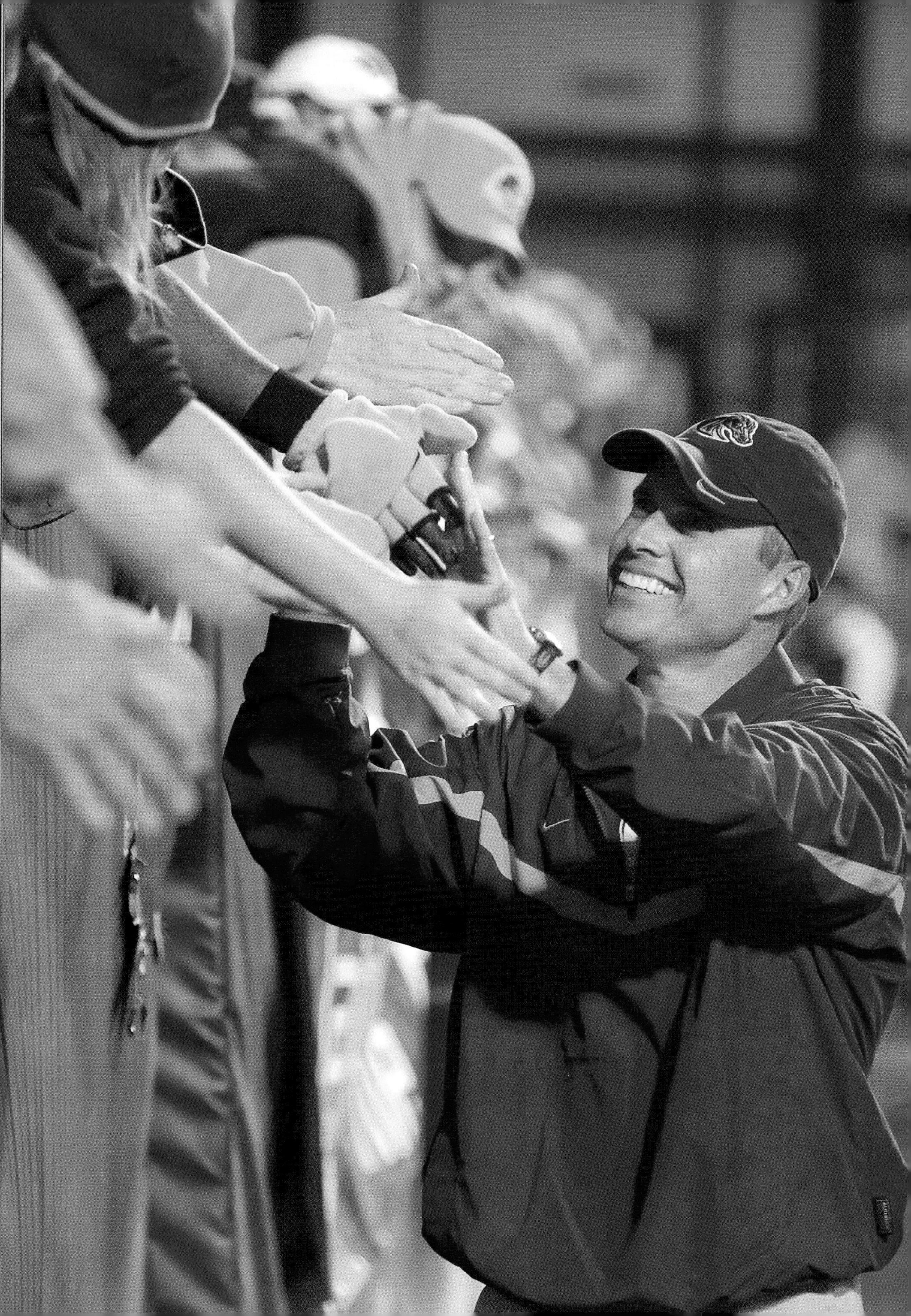

LA Tech kicker Danny Horwedel's field goal is blocked in the second quarter. *Stanley Brewster/Arbiter*

The first BSU points came after a nine-play, 76-yard drive. Quarterback Jared Zabransky capped off the drive with a two-yard option keeper to even the score at 7-7. The first Bronco drive took just 3:42 and was based around the running of Ian Johnson and Vinny Perretta. Johnson broke a 29-yard run on the drive. Perretta broke a 17-yard run of his own on the fourth play of the series.

The second LA Tech offensive possession showed little sign of life. LA Tech was forced to punt after three consecutive incomplete passes by Zac Champion. Boise State took over on its own 34-yard line but was held to three plays and a punt. On the ensuing Bronco punt the ball bounced off the back of LA Tech corner Anthony Moss.

Head coach Chris Petersen greets Boise State fans following his team's win over LA Tech. *Stanley Brewster/Arbiter*

It appeared Moss had no idea he was near the bouncing ball when it hit him. Boise State linebacker Josh Bean recovered the muffed punt, which set up the Bronco offense at the Bulldog 28-yard line.

It would only take six plays for BSU to find the end zone for the second time of the night. Ian Johnson punched in a two-yard run to give the Broncos a 14-7 lead after the first quarter.

Boise State continued to capitalize on short LA Tech offensive drives. BSU racked up 17 points in the second quarter, which kept the Bulldog defense on its heels all night long. Zabransky found Drisan James for a 42-yard reception to put the Broncos deep in Bulldog territory at the 23-yard line. Zabransky finished off the drive with a one-yard keeper just 2:15 into the second quarter.

	1st	2nd	3rd	4th	Final
Louisiana Tech	7	0	0	7	14
Boise State	14	17	17	7	55

Scoring Summary

1st

TECH: Jackson 1-yard run (Horwedel kick)—4 plays, 14 yards in 1:49.

BSU: Zabransky 2-yard run (Montgomery kick)—9 plays, 76 yards in 3:42.

BSU: I. Johnson 2-yard run (Montgomery kick)—6 plays, 28 yards in 2:13.

2nd

BSU: Zabransky 1-yard run (Montgomery kick)—6 plays, 87 yards in 1:37.

BSU: Rabb 5-yard pass from Zabransky (Montgomery kick)—8 plays, 76 yards in 3:34.

BSU: Montgomery 30-yard field goal—9 plays, 65 yards in 2:52.

3rd

BSU: Denton 24-yard pass from Zabransky (Montgomery kick)—4 plays, 59 yards in 1:11.

BSU: Montgomery 39-yard field goal—6 plays, 25 yards in 2:50.

BSU: Tadman 98-yard interception return (Montgomery kick)

4th

BSU: Denton 1-yard run (Montgomery kick)—15 plays, 80 yards in 8:38.

TECH: Porter 10-yard run (Horwedel kick)—4 plays, 38 yards in 1:02.

Team Statistics

	TECH	BSU
First Downs	20	24
Rushes-Yards (Net)	141	265
Passing Yards (Net)	163	224
Passes (Comp-Att-Int)	17-35-1	15-23-0
Total Offense (Plays-Yards)	70-304	65-489
Fumble Returns-Yards	0-0	0-0
Punt Returns-Yards	1-1	3-5
Kickoff Returns-Yards	9-184	2-38
Interception-Yards	0-0	1-98
Punts (Number-Yards)	7-261	1-34
Fumbles-Lost	1-1	3-3
Sacks By (Number-Yards)	0-0	3-33
Penalties-Yards	9-80	6-62
Possession Time	30:46	29:14

Zabransky found Jerard Rabb for a five-yard touchdown pass to give the Broncos a 28-7 lead in the second. Rabb was flagged twice following the play for excessive celebration and was tossed from the game by ruling on the double flag.

Rabb led the team in receiving with four catches for 48 yards and a score, despite only playing one and a half quarters. Anthony Montgomery finished off the first half with a 30-yard field goal to give the Broncos their 31-7 halftime lead.

The second half went in a similar fashion for both teams as Boise State jumped back on the scoreboard just over five minutes into the second half. Zabransky found Brett Denton for his second touchdown pass of the game.

Denton scored on a screen pass that broke open into a 24-yard touchdown run. Denton scored again in the fourth quarter on a one-yard run that capped a 15-play drive for the Bronco second string.

Boise State safety Marty Tadman provided the play of the night, intercepting La Tech quarterback Zac Champion on the BSU two-yard line.

Tadman returned the pick 98 yards up the right sideline for a touchdown. The interception was Tadman's second of the year.

"That's longer than I've run in a long time," Tadman said. "The guys, Kyle Gingg and Quinton Jones, blocking up there, that was the only reason I got there. I got tired about 60 yards into it."

LA Tech scored a touchdown with less than a minute to play to close the gap slightly.

Broncos safety Marty Tadman (20) is hoisted by a teammate after he returned an interception 98 yards for a touchdown.
Stanley Brewster/Arbiter

However, the final score showed just how well the Broncos could avoid any midseason letdowns.

"I think if you put the work in during the week and you know what you're doing, you prepare in your mind as you go," Petersen said. "We just don't believe around here you can show up excited on Saturday and play good."

Offensively, Zabransky and Johnson led Boise State.

Zabransky threw just 18 passes, but completed 11 for 184 yards. He also threw two touchdown passes and scored two rushing touchdowns. Johnson rushed the ball 14 times on limited carries for 92 yards.

"If we continue to give that guy (Johnson) the ball 30 times every game he might not be with us for the whole entire season," Petersen said. "We need to feed that guy. We're gonna continue to do that."

Korey Hall led the BSU defense with nine tackles for the night. Tadman chipped in with seven tackles to go along with his interception return. The Bronco defense forced seven punts by Louisiana Tech.

Boise State travels to New Mexico State Sunday, October 15. The Broncos will look to extend their record to 7-0 and continue moving up the national rankings. New Mexico State is 2-3 for the season, 0-1 in Western Athletic Conference play.

Stanley Brewster Arbiter

BOISE STATE OUTLASTS HOLBROOK AND THE AGGIES OFFENSE

BY KYE JOHNSON

A win is a win.

The Boise State Broncos found that out October 15 against a feisty New Mexico State team that didn't want to go away. The Broncos defensive secondary had some troubles against Aggie quarterback Chase Holbrook, giving up 526 yards through the air.

"We just didn't compete as best we could and we just didn't play up to our standards," Bronco safety Gerald Alexander said. "But New Mexico State has a good offense, they're a potent team and you got to tip your hat off to them. But we know we can play better."

Boise State got off to a good start as Holbrook threw an interception to linebacker Korey Hall on his second attempt of the game. Hall's interception set up a seven-yard Ian Johnson touchdown run to give Boise State a 7-0 lead. On the next Aggie possession, the Bronco defense forced a three-and-out and set up the offense with great field position again. Quarterback Jared Zabransky immediately went to a play-action pass for a 34-yard gain to Jerard Rabb all the way inside the Aggie 10-yard line. Johnson again finished off the drive, this time from a yard out.

On New Mexico State's third possession, receiver A.J. Harris fumbled the ball, which the Broncos recovered. The Bronco offense then went on

Colt Brooks and Dennis Ellis celebrate after a big defensive play.
Stanley Brewste/Arbiter.

64

a nine-play, 50-yard touchdown drive. The drive was capped off by another Johnson touchdown run. Johnson finished the first quarter with 36 yards on nine carries and three touchdowns.

Early in the second quarter, the Aggies showed a little life as safety Eric Carrie intercepted a Zabransky pass intended for Legedu Naanee. Once again the Bronco defense was stiff and forced a 38-yard field goal attempt. Aggie sophomore kicker Matt Pratt sent his kick wide left and the Broncos kept their 21-point lead.

Holbrook and the Aggie offense finally got hot mid-way through the second quarter on a 12-play, 84-yard drive. Running back Jeremiah Williams finished off the drive with a three-yard touchdown plunge.

The Broncos struck back with 3:34 remaining in the first half as Johnson scored his fourth rushing touchdown. This time it was from 17 yards out. Before the half could end, Holbrook and the quick-strike Aggie offense got some points on the board.

Holbrook hooked up with Derek Dubois for a 65-yard touchdown pass. The Aggies got the ball back with under a minute remaining and drove into Bronco territory. With 0:02 seconds left in the half and the ball on the Boise State 24, the Aggies chose to throw the ball into the end zone rather than attempt a 41-yard field goal. Holbrook was pressured hard and his pass was intercepted by safety Marty Tadman, which brought an entertaining first half to a close.

> "WE JUST DIDN'T COMPETE AS BEST WE COULD AND WE JUST DIDN'T PLAY UP TO OUR STANDARDS."
>
> BSU SAFETY GERALD ALEXANDER

Even though Boise State held a 27-14 halftime lead, it was apparent the Aggie no-huddle offense was starting to go into effect against the Bronco secondary.

"That's one of the more difficult things," Alexander said. "That's one thing I didn't really expect, the no-huddle offense the whole game. It's difficult because they line up and you're searching for what defense you're going to run and stuff like that."

The Bronco offense started the second half in anything but stellar fashion, immediately going 3-and-out. The Aggie offense wasted no time before going to work. Holbrook led the Aggies down the field and into Bronco territory on their first drive of the second half. Faced with a fourth and 10, Holbrook found Dubois over the middle, who slipped a tackle and ran the ball inside the Bronco five-yard line. Holbrook kept the ball himself from a yard out later in the series to bring New Mexico State within six points at the 9:19 mark of the third quarter.

Suddenly, it was a game again. Facing a huge third and nine on the next Bronco possession, Zabransky completed a 19-yard pass to Rabb to keep the drive alive. On the same drive, facing a fourth down, Zabransky threw a pass over the middle that was dropped by Drisan

Broncos wideout Jerard Rabb pulls in a deep pass from Jared Zabransky. *Stanley Brewster/Arbiter*

66

	1st	2nd	3rd	4th	Final
Boise State	21	6	6	7	**40**
New Mexico State	0	14	7	7	**28**

Scoring Summary

1st

BSU: I. Johnson 7-yard run (Montgomery kick)—6 plays, 26 yards in 2:55.

BSU: I. Johnson 1-yard run (Montgomery kick)—3 plays, 40 yards in 1:09.

BSU: I. Johnson 3-yard run (Montgomery kick)—9 plays, 50 yards in 2:58.

2nd

NMSU: Williams 3-yard run (Pratt kick)—12 plays, 82 yards in 4:19.

BSU: I. Johnson 17-yard run (Montgomery kick failed)—6 plays, 76 yards in 2:30.

NMSU: Dubois 65-yard pass from Holbrook (Pratt kick)—4 plays, 66 yards in 2:01.

3rd

NMSU: Holbrook 1-yard run (Pratt kick)—13 plays, 71 yards in 3:14.

BSU: Childs 22-yard pass from Zabransky (Zabransky pass failed)—10 plays, 84 yards in 4:23.

4th

BSU: Perretta 33-yard pass from Zabransky (Montgomery kick)—5 plays, 80 yards in 2:51.

NMSU: Williams 7-yard pass from Holbrook (Pratt kick)—16 plays, 80 yards in 7:22.

Team Statistics

	BSU	NMSU
First Downs	23	28
Rushes-Yards (Net)	255	8
Passing Yards (Net)	215	526
Passes (Comp-Att-Int)	14-21-1	49-65-2
Total Offense (Plays-Yards)	63-470	85-534
Fumble Returns-Yards	0-0	0-0
Punt Returns-Yards	1-20	1-0
Kickoff Returns-Yards	4-67	4-50
Interception-Yards	2-74	1-0
Punts (Number-Yards)	2-83	2-71
Fumbles-Lost	1-1	2-1
Sacks By (Number-Yards)	4-21	0-0
Penalties-Yards	6-55	7-64
Possession Time	28:26	31:34

James. However, the Broncos were bailed out by a roughing-the-passer penalty, which kept the possession going. Zabransky ultimately hooked up with Jeremy Childs for a 22-yard touchdown pass in the back corner of the end zone. Boise State tried for the two-point conversion rather than kick the extra point and failed.

With 1:04 remaining, New Mexico State made a decision to try a 30-yard field goal, a decision head coach Hal Mumme would probably like to take back. Pratt, the struggling Aggie kicker, got his 30-yard attempt blocked.

"They had things moving and we were struggling," Bronco linebacker Colt Brooks said. "It was a great thing we got in there and we were able to stop the play and show them we were still there. It was a great play and it boosted our morale too."

Boise State cashed in on the golden opportunity with a 33-yard touchdown pass from Zabransky to Vinny Perretta on the ensuing drive. Perretta had a birthday Saturday, and all he wanted was a touchdown.

The touchdown gave Boise State a little breathing room, extending the lead to 40-21 with more than 13 minutes to play.

The Aggies refused to give in completely, however. Holbrook drove the Aggie offense down field and found Chris Williams for a seven-yard touchdown with 5:47 remaining. Williams tallied more than 150 yards receiving with the catch, the first Aggie to do so since November 16, 1974.

Junior kicker Ryan Bowling attempted the extra point, rather than Pratt. Bowling converted and brought the score to within 12 points with

The Boise State offense receives on-field instructions from the coach. *Stanley Brewster/Arbiter*

5:47 to go. Pratt did come out on the ensuing kickoff to attempt the onside kick that Boise State eventually recovered.

A steady diet of Johnson and Brett Denton on the Broncos' last possession ran the clock down to 15 seconds before Holbrook completed two meaningless passes to end the game. The Broncos improved to 7-0 on the season (3-0 Western Athletic Conference), and New Mexico State dropped to 2-4 (0-2 WAC).

A little side note to go along with the game was the Bowl Championship Series rankings being released. Coach Chris Peterson didn't want to talk about where the Broncos were ranked and said he wasn't concerned, but the Broncos came in at No. 15 in the first rankings of the season.

GOVERNOR'S CUP EXCEEDS EXPECTATIONS

BY JAKE GARCIN

The beautiful thing about college football rivalries: no game between two rivals goes as planned. Regardless of how good a team is supposed to be and how bad the other is expected to play, a rivalry game almost always gives the unexpected.

The October 21 match-up between Boise State and the University of Idaho was no exception. Nationally ranked Boise State (No. 17) found itself in a hole early in Moscow after Vandal quarterback Steven Wichman found Wendell Octave for a four-yard touchdown pass. The score capped off a nine-play, 86-yard drive and gave Idaho a 7-0 lead just 4:50 into the game.

The Vandals narrowly escaped a huge momentum swing after Octave fumbled the football on the opening play of the

> "I EXPECT THEM TO GO OUT AND COMPETE HARD AND DO THEIR BEST."
>
> BSU HEAD COACH
> CHRIS PETERSEN

game. Idaho managed to recover the fumble and capitalized one play later. Running back Brian Flowers turned a screen pass into a 48-yard gain to put Idaho deep in Bronco territory. Seven plays

Boise State quarterback Jared Zabransky looks to the sideline during the game against Idaho.
Stanley Brewster/Arbiter

Broncos cornerback Rashaun Scott wraps up the Idaho ball carrier. *Stanley Brewster/Arbiter*

later Boise State found itself down 7-0 and its defense reeling from the quick Vandal passing attack.

After a three-and-out by the Bronco offense, Idaho was in business once again. The Vandals pulled out their second big play of the day, a 45-yard gain, that set up a 41-yard field goal attempt by Tino Amancio. BSU got its first break of the game as Amancio's kick sailed wide left.

BSU went to its running game on their second drive. Ian Johnson picked up six yards on the first play of the drive. Vinny Perretta followed up Johnson with a nine-yard run to pick up the first down. The small success on the ground helped to silence the Vandal fans and build some momentum for Boise State. Three plays

later Bronco quarterback Jared Zabransky found Legedu Naanee on a slant across the middle for a 61-yard touchdown pitch-and-catch. Naanee threw Vandal safety Shiloh Keo to the ground with a stiff-arm after that catch, which sprung him for the big-play score.

"(That) was huge," Zabransky said. "Their safety didn't get over the top so I put it right in that hole and he made a great play. He's just a lot bigger than what they had out there."

Despite the offensive answer from the Broncos, Idaho's offense continued to roll. Wichman led the Vandal offense back down the field on an 11-play drive where he found tight-end Luke Smith-Anderson for an 18-yard touchdown pass. The score gave the Vandals the lead for the second time on the day. The touchdown came with just 1:04 to go in the first quarter, ending an exciting first period in the Kibbie Dome.

Boise State's defense cleaned up its play in the second quarter, holding the Vandals scoreless for the rest of the first half. BSU's offense also continued to gain momentum in the second quarter. The first Boise State possession of the second quarter resulted in an eight-play, 58-yard drive. Ian Johnson scored his first rushing touchdown of the game with 10:22 to go in the half, tying the score 14-14.

BSU extended its lead to 21-14 with another touchdown on their next offensive possession. Zabransky found Jerard Rabb midway through the drive for a 39-yard reception. Zabransky then found tight end Derek Schouman on a three-yard strike into the end zone for a 21-14 lead at the half.

The Broncos received the opening kickoff of the second half and looked to be moving into position to put away the Vandals. However, after a three and out by the BSU offense, Idaho quickly moved down the field and set up Amancio for a 29-yard field goal. The field goal pulled Idaho to 21-17 and gave a new shot of life into the Vandal attack.

"If we don't make those stupid little mistakes, we probably put that game away a little sooner,"

> "IF WE DON'T MAKE THOSE STUPID LITTLE MISTAKES, WE PROBABLY PUT THAT GAME AWAY A LITTLE SOONER. NO ONE PANICKED. WE'VE DONE THAT A COUPLE TIMES."
>
> BSU RUNNING BACK
> IAN JOHNSON

Johnson said. "No one panicked. We've done that a couple times."

Boise State was able to maintain its poise throughout an offensive drought in the third quarter and a scary start to the fourth quarter. BSU did find a small rhythm on its second drive of the third quarter. Behind the running of Johnson, the Broncos marched down to the Idaho 18-yard line. On the ensuing play Johnson patiently broke off the left tackle and cut back to the middle of the field for his second touchdown of the day.

With a 28-17 deficit to overcome, Idaho refused to give up and continued to chip away at the Bronco defense with dump passes and run plays at the middle of the BSU defensive line. The Vandals narrowed the gap 28-20 with a second Amancio field goal. Amancio knocked the 25-yard attempt dead center with just 1:30 to play in the third.

The fourth quarter provided nervous moments for Bronco fans, as Zabransky was sacked for an 18-yard loss at his own seven-yard line. On the next Vandal possession Wichman converted a third-and-eight and a third-and-nine to keep the Idaho drive alive. Wichman threw his third touchdown of the day with just 7:05 in the game. Wichman found Marlon Haynes on a 41-yard touchdown pass to close the gap to two points, 28-26. Vandal head

	1st	2nd	3rd	4th	Final
Boise State	7	14	7	14	42
University of Idaho	14	0	6	6	26

Scoring Summary

1st

UI: Octave 4-yard pass from Wichman (Amancio kick)—9 plays, 86 yards in 4:50.

BSU: Naanee 61-yard pass from Zabransky (Montgomery kick)—5 plays, 76 yards in 2:13.

UI: Smith 18-yard pass from Wichman (Amancio kick)—11 plays, 80 yards in 4:00

2nd

BSU: I. Johnson 8-yard run (Montgomery kick)—8 plays, 58 yards in 3:00.

BSU: Schouman 3-yard pass from Zabransky (Montgomery kick)—9 plays, 71 yards in 4:09.

3rd

UI: Amancio 29-yard field goal—7 plays, 12 yards in 2:50.

BSU: I. Johnson 18-yard run (Montgomery kick)—7 plays, 78 yards in 3:23.

UI: Amancio 25-yard field goal—4 plays, 4 yards in 2:01.

4th

UI: Haynes 41-yard pass from Wichman (Wichman pass failed)—7 plays, 66 yards in 3:02.

BSU: I. Johnson 4-yard run (Montgomery kick)—5 plays, 25 yards in 1:44.

BSU: I. Johnson 12-yard run (Montgomery kick)—4 plays, 44 yards in 1:41.

Team Statistics

	BSU	UI
First Downs	17	20
Rushes-Yards (Net)	208	69
Passing Yards (Net)	145	328
Passes (Comp-Att-Int)	10-23-1	24-45-2
Total Offense (Plays-Yards)	60-353	73-397
Fumble Returns-Yards	0-0	0-0
Punt Returns-Yards	4-23	4-47
Kickoff Returns-Yards	4-104	4-62
Interception-Yards	2-19	1-35
Punts (Number-Yards)	6-213	5-214
Fumbles-Lost	3-0	1-0
Sacks By (Number-Yards)	1-12	1-17
Penalties-Yards	5-50	8-67
Possession Time	28:50	31:10

coach Dennis Erickson elected to go for the two-point conversion. Idaho was denied when Orlando Scandrick laid out to knock down a pass in the back of the end zone to keep the BSU lead at 28-26.

On the next kickoff by Idaho, Boise State found the last spark they would need to close the doors on the Vandals. After an afternoon of "sky-kicks" by the Vandals to avoid big special teams plays, BSU's Rashaun Scott fielded a short kick and returned it 42 yards up the Boise State sideline. To add insult to injury, Idaho was also charged with a late hit penalty, which added 15 yards to the end of the run.

"That's stuff we've worked on since day one of training camp," BSU head coach Chris Petersen said. "Finally it came to fruition. That's why we've got him back there. We have a lot of guys like that, that kind of hide behind the spotlight and when they get a chance they can make plays."

The return by Scott set up another Ian Johnson touchdown with 5:02 to play. The Boise State defense forced a turnover on downs on the next Idaho drive, which led to Johnson's fourth and final touchdown of the game. The 12-yard run by Johnson gave the Broncos a 42-26 lead, which would be the final score of the 35th Governor's Cup.

Johnson finished the game with 183 rushing yards on 27 carries. The majority of Johnson's work came after the first quarter. Ian carried the ball just three times in the first quarter for nine yards. As the game progressed, however, so did Johnson's involvement on the field.

Head coach Chris Petersen is presented with the Governor's Cup following Boise State's 42-26 win over Idaho.
Stanley Brewster/Arbiter

On defense BSU was led once again by senior linebacker Korey Hall. Hall led the team in tackles (nine), solo tackles (seven) and also recorded one interception.

As a whole the Bronco defense allowed 328 passing yards and three passing touchdowns. For the second consecutive week the BSU defense showed weakness in its pass coverage. However, the Broncos enter a 10-day break before hosting the Fresno State Bulldogs, which will give Coach Petersen plenty of time to right the wrongs on defense.

"There's a lot of expectations surrounding this team and people expect us to go out and win with a certain way and a certain style," Petersen said. "I expect them to go out and compete hard and do their best. When you're playing in someone else's house, to get out and win like we did, I'm proud of those guys."

SIT, ROLL OVER, GOOD BULLDOG, NOW GO HOME

BY JAKE GARCIN

As the saying goes, there's a first time for everything. Boise State's football game against Fresno State had plenty of firsts. The Broncos had yet to play a Wednesday night game this season. It was also the first time Bronco Stadium was choreographed for national television. BSU fans executed a request for people in odd-numbered sections to wear orange and even-numbered sections to wear blue.

"I want to say how much I appreciate our fans," BSU head coach Chris Petersen said following the game. "(We appreciate) how much energy they bring to the stadium, doing the blue-orange out. I'm always amazed that 30,000 people seems like 75,000 people to me. All the guys in the program really appreciate what (the fans) do for us."

One first that wouldn't be seen November 1 was Boise State's first loss of the season. The Broncos improved their record to 9-0 (5-0 Western Athletic Conference) on the year, defeating Fresno State 45-21. The Bulldogs fell to 1-7 (1-3 WAC) on the season losing their seventh consecutive game this year.

> "I DON'T KNOW HOW THEY JUDGE US OR WHAT DECIDES IF WE GO TO A BCS GAME OR NOT. ALL WE CAN DO IS GO OUT AND TRY AND WIN GAMES."
>
> BSU LINEBACKER
> KOREY HALL

Tim Brady (24) helps teammates tackle a Fresno State player.
Stanley Brewster/Arbiter

It took the Boise State offense 10:33 and a punt fake to finally get rolling. After being forced to punt on its second possession of the game, BSU ran a direct-snap play to Legedu Naanee, who picked up 30 yards on the fake punt. The Broncos converted a 38-yard Anthony Montgomery field goal four plays later, putting the Broncos on the scoreboard first. The field goal came with 4:27 to go in the first quarter.

On the ensuing kickoff, Fresno State kick returner Chastin West took Montgomery's kickoff 93 yards for the first Fresno touchdown of the game. The touchdown gave Fresno a 7-3 lead, but seemed to act as the spark Boise State needed to catch fire. The Bronco offense ran off 21 unanswered points to end the half. The first Bronco touchdown came with just seven seconds left in the first quarter. Jared Zabransky found Drisan James for a 28-yard hookup and a 10-7 lead after a quarter of play.

Zabransky threw his second touchdown pass of the game on the first Boise State offensive drive of the second quarter. Zabransky found Vinny Perretta on an eight-yard swing pass to extend the BSU lead to 17-7. The score came after an 11-play, 52-yard drive. Zabransky was named player of the game, finishing the night 19-25 for 180 yards, three touchdowns and one interception. He also rushed for 57 yards on 11 carries.

BSU running back Ian Johnson found the end zone for his 19th score of the year just 2:23 before halftime. Johnson followed fullback Brad Lau on a three-yard pitch to the left side of the field. Johnson finished the half with 64 rushing yards on 16 carries.

The Bulldogs started the second half with their first real offensive production of the game. Following a 22-yard run by Dwayne Wright, Fresno found its way down to the Boise State 40-yard line. The BSU defense held strong, however, forcing the fourth Bulldog punt of the game. Jerard Rabb provided a 43-yard reception to get BSU into Fresno State territory. Rabb was rewarded six plays later as Zabransky found Rabb for a four-yard touchdown pass.

On the next Fresno possession Boise State linebacker Korey Hall picked off Tom Brandstater and returned the ball 22 yards to the Fresno State 10-yard line. The interception was Hall's sixth of the season. Hall also chipped in with five tackles on the night.

Despite the 38-7 deficit Fresno refused to quit, scoring again with 1:40 to play. Brandstater found Joe Fernandez for a 20-yard touchdown catch after a miscommunication in the Bronco secondary between Marty Tadman and Orlando Scandrick.

On the next BSU drive Damon Jenkins intercepted Zabransky. Jenkins returned the pick 56 yards for a touchdown. The score narrowed the gap to 38-21 but would be the closest Fresno could manage to get. The BSU defense forced a Fresno punt on the first Bulldog drive of the fourth quarter.

Ian Johnson capped the game off with his second touchdown of the night. Johnson broke open a 32-yard run to set the Broncos up on the Fresno two-yard line. Johnson's two-yard

Mike Dominguez (74) carries the sledgehammer onto the field alongside teammates Tristan Patin (16) and Anthony Montgomery (47). *Stanley Brewster/Arbiter*

	1st	2nd	3rd	4th	Final
Fresno State	7	0	7	7	21
Boise State	10	14	14	7	45

Scoring Summary

1st

BSU: Montgomery 38-yard field goal–9 plays, 50 yards in 3:41.

FS: West 93-yard kickoff return (Stitser kick)

BSU: James 28-yard pass from Zabransky (Montgomery kick)–8 plays, 72 yards in 4:02.

2nd

BSU: Perretta 4-yard run (Montgomery kick)–3 plays, 9 yards in 1:40.

BSU: I. Johnson 3-yard run (Montgomery kick)–13 plays, 60 yards in 4:09.

3rd

BSU: Rabb 4-yard pass from Zabransky (Montgomery kick)–8 plays, 92 yards in 3:52.

BSU: Perretta 4-yard run (Montgomery kick)–3 plays, 9 yards in 1:40.

FS: Fernandez 20-yard pass from Brandstater (Stitser kick)–9 plays, 62 yards in 4:45.

4th

FS: Jenkins 56-yard interception return (Stitser kick)

BSU: I. Johnson 2-yard run (Montgomery kick)–5 plays, 53 yards in 2:30.

Team Statistics

	FS	BSU
First Downs	11	23
Rushing Yards (Net)	102	300
Passing Yards (Net)	121	180
Passes (Comp-Att-Int)	12-24-1	19-25-1
Total Offense (Plays-Yards)	50-223	72-480
Fumble Returns-Yards	0-0	0-0
Punt Returns-Yards	1-0	1-1
Kickoff Returns-Yards	7-178	3-70
Interception-Yards	1-56	1-22
Punts (Number-Yards)	5-168	2-98
Fumbles-Lost	0-0	0-0
Sacks By (Number-Yards)	2-7	2-12
Penalties-Yards	5-42	5-31
Possession Time	25:10	34:50

touchdown run solidified another standout performance for the sophomore back. He finished with 139 rushing yards on 24 carries and only three negative rushing yards.

Johnson took advantage of another nationally televised game. He was announced as the fourth player on the Heisman watch list by ESPN earlier Wednesday. With Boise State fans waving Heisman promotional posters, Johnson did his part to prove the hype is well deserved.

"That guy just pounds away and pounds away," Zabransky said. "It doesn't look like he's getting much and (he'll) spring it. He's so slippery and has great balance. He does a great job in reading his blocks. He's a workhorse and we're going to keep riding that workhorse until the end of the season. He's very deserving of all the attention he's getting."

Kyle Wilson led the Broncos defensively. The freshman from Piscataway, New Jersey, led the team with 11 tackles, eight of which were solo. Wilson was suspended for the season's first three games after an undisclosed team violation. Wilson has worked his way back into the cornerback rotation since then and appeared to have his breakout game. Fresno attempted to throw at Wilson and test the youngster early and often. Wilson proved he was game by giving the best performance of his young collegiate career.

"I was pretty anxious," Wilson said. "I just wanted to represent the East coast. Go out there and make some plays. I've got 10 messages on my phone and I haven't checked yet. I think everyone (back home) stayed up and watched it."

Quarterback Jared Zabransky hands the ball off to running back Brett Denton. *Stanley Brewster/Arbiter*

With just three games remaining on the 2006 schedule the Broncos are moving closer to the coveted Bowl Championship Series bid with every win. Two Tostitos Fiesta Bowl representatives were in attendance, which bodes well for the Broncos' future. There were also representatives for the Orange Bowl in attendance.

"I don't know how they judge us or what decides if we go to a BCS game or not," Korey Hall said. "All we can do is go out and try and win games. (If) we score as many points as possible and not let them score very many, I think they'll figure it out."

The Broncos travel to San Jose State on November 11 for a game that ESPN announced would be televised nationally.

HUMBLE JOHNSON CLIMBS HEISMAN LADDER

BY KYE JOHNSON

As the Boise State football team continues to creep its way higher and higher in the national polls and rankings, Bronco running back Ian Johnson's name continues to get thrown around more seriously in the Heisman talk.

The shifty sophomore from San Dimas, California, leads the nation with 20 rushing touchdowns. He also ranks second in the nation with 1,317 rushing yards. The "Johnson for Heisman" talk is being thrown around all over the country, ranging from ESPN.com (where he is currently on their "Heisman Watch List") to some CBS sportsline voters who publicly have Johnson ranked as high as third in their polls.

Even with all the buzz going around, Johnson continues to remain humble.

"People know way more about it than I do," Johnson said. "I don't read the newspaper anymore. I don't watch TV. I just stay in my own little bubble. It's great for my family. It's great for the team, great for the city. It's not me that got that; it's the team. I'm just part of that team. Without the defense, without the lineman, without my wide receivers making blocks, none of this would have happened. I just happen to be the person whose name is attached to it, since they can't say the Boise State Broncos are up for Heisman."

That all may be true, but Johnson's performances—particularly his performances on national television—have him listed among the Heisman hopefuls. Currently, most polls show Ohio State quarterback Troy Smith leading the race with a trio of players behind him. Most lists include Johnson, Rutgers running back Ray Rice, West Virginia running back Steve Slaton, and Notre Dame quarterback Brady Quinn.

"I didn't even know my name was in the Heisman at first. That shows how much I was paying attention. Then to have it mentioned with me, that's the biggest honor to me ever," said Johnson. "It's one of those things where I know there's five other dudes out there who deserve their name on it also, and those are my linemen."

In BSU's most recent game against Fresno State, flyers made their way around Bronco

Heisman candidate Ian Johnson, only a sophomore, runs the ball against Hawaii.
Stanley Brewster/Arbiter

Stadium promoting Johnson and his Heisman campaign.

"I loved it," Johnson said. "I actually didn't notice it until someone threw one from the top row and it hit me. I was like, 'What is this, an airplane?' Then I opened it up and I was like 'Whoa, that's sweet!'"

Boise State has played three games already this season on ESPN, and Johnson has performed well in each of those games.

In all three games the Bronco offense has given the ball to Johnson at least 22 times and he has rushed for a total of 11 touchdowns. Johnson's 11 touchdowns in three ESPN games is more than the second rushing scorer in the WAC. Hawaii 's Nate Ilaoa is the No. 2 rushing scorer this year with only eight touchdowns for the entire season.

But despite all of his success, Johnson is not the front runner to win the award.

However, if he continues to perform well on national television for the remainder of the year he may at least make the trip to New York for the awards banquet, which is annually held at the Downtown Athletic Club in New York City.

"I've never been to New York, so I think I'd enjoy it," Johnson said. "It would be the highlight of my career to this point, and I'd enjoy every moment of it. It's not one of those things that if it doesn't happen, I'm like, 'Wow, I failed myself.' It's not one of my goals. All my goals, I have the team involved. I don't want to put

myself before anyone. If the team does well and there's no Heisman, that doesn't matter."

Boise State has two remaining games to be shown on ESPN, the first against San Jose State and its regular-season finale against Nevada.

"It's one of those things. If anything it would be an honor for my team more so than me."

Ian Johnson celebrates alongside teammates after a big play during the regular season.
Stanley Brewster/Arbiter

BOISE STATE WINS NAIL BITER 23-20

BY JAKE GARCIN

B oise State football fans experienced a feeling of déjà vu November 11.

The Broncos found themselves tied 20-20 with the San Jose Spartans with only 12 seconds left in the game. Two years ago the Broncos were undefeated and ranked No. 13 in the country when they entered Spartan Stadium. After an offensive shootout BSU escaped the 2004 game with a 56-49 double-overtime win.

"I love this place," Boise State head coach Chris Petersen said following the game. "It brings out our guys' competitive spirits. It shows what we're really made of. Our backs were to the wall most of the game, but they came through like champions."

This year's BSU team entered the game 9-0 and ranked No. 14 in the country. San Jose managed to hold the Broncos scoreless in the first

> "I LOVE THIS PLACE. IT BRINGS OUT OUR GUYS' COMPETITIVE SPIRITS. IT SHOWS WHAT WE'RE REALLY MADE OF. OUR BACKS WERE TO THE WALL MOST OF THE GAME, BUT THEY CAME THROUGH LIKE CHAMPIONS."
>
> BCS HEAD COACH
> CHRIS PETERSEN

Colt Brooks drags down San Jose State quarterback Adam Tafralis.
Stanley Brewster/Arbiter

quarter and out of the end zone for the entire first half. It was the first time all season the Broncos were shut out after a quarter of play. It was also the first time all year BSU failed to score a touchdown in the first half.

With just under three minutes left in the game it appeared as if BSU was headed for another overtime game in San Jose. Marty Tadman changed that notion with a 44-yard punt return all the way down to the San Jose 37-yard line. Tadman set up the Bronco offense with one last chance to score with 2:33 on the clock.

"There was a lot of room to run," Tadman said. "There was great blocking up front. I think I was back there to play it safe, catch the ball, and get the offense on the field. It turned out to be more than that."

On the game's final drive BSU quarterback Jared Zabransky found Vinny Perretta for a 10-yard completion that moved the Broncos down to the 26-yard line. Three plays later BSU was sitting at the 19-yard line with two seconds left on the game clock and their Bowl Championship Series dreams riding on the leg of Anthony Montgomery.

Montgomery drove home the 37-yard attempt as time expired and Boise State moved up on the scoreboard 23-20. The win came in the most dramatic fashion of the season as Montgomery kicked his first career game-winning field goal.

Montgomery was 3-for-3 on field goal attempts for the game. BSU scored on two field goals in the second quarter.

Montgomery split the uprights from 24 yards out to cap a 13-play, 83-yard drive.

Boise State would settle for its second field goal of the game with just 12 seconds left to play in the first half. After marching down to the San Jose six-yard line, BSU was held to no gain on the following two plays. Quarterback Jared Zabransky was sacked for a four-yard loss, forcing a 27-yard field goal by Montgomery. Montgomery's second made field goal closed the gap to 7-6 to end the first half of play.

San Jose found its only score of the first half on a 10-yard touchdown pass from Adam Tafralis to James Jones. Jones caught the pass on a fade route to the right corner of the end zone. The one touchdown was all San Jose needed to become the first team all season to lead the Broncos at halftime.

It took BSU 8:05 in the second half to take its first lead of the game, 12-7. Zabransky found Drisan James on a 43-yard hook up down the middle of the field to put the Broncos at the 11-yard line. San Jose was able to hold BSU to a fourth and goal on the two-yard line. The Spartans failed to make a final stand, however, as running back Ian Johnson found the end zone for the first time all game on a two-yard touchdown run. BSU opted to go for a two-point conversion but was stopped on a Zabransky interception at the goal line.

On the ensuing San Jose drive the Spartans recaptured the lead on a four-yard touchdown

Kyle Stringer (42) celebrates with kicker Anthony Montgomery after Montgomery's game-winning field goal.
Stanley Brewster/Arbiter

	1st	2nd	3rd	4th	Final
Boise State	0	6	6	11	23
San Jose State	0	7	6	7	20

Scoring Summary

2nd

SJSU: Jones 10-yard pass from Tafralis (Strubeck kick)—9 plays, 70 yards in 4:59.

BSU: Montgomery 24-yard field goal—13 plays, 83 yards in 7:36.

BSU: Montgomery 27-yard field goal—9 plays, 59 yards in 4:05.

3rd

BSU: I. Johnson 2-yard run (Zabransky pass intercepted)—9 plays, 81 yards in 4:37.

SJSU: Broussard 4-yard pass from Tafralis (Davis pass failed)—10 plays, 67 yards in 5:34.

4th

SJSU: Jones 3-yard pass from Tafralis (Strubeck kick)—3 plays, 5 yards in 1:16.

BSU: Zabransky 1-yard run (Rabb pass from Zabransky)—12 plays, 63 yards in 5:16.

BSU: Montgomery 37-yard field goal—7 plays, 18 yards in 2:33.

Team Statistics

	BSU	SJSU
First Downs	20	13
Rushing Yards (Net)	160	75
Passing Yards (Net)	181	173
Passes (Comp-Att-Int)	14-20-1	17-23-0
Total Offense (Plays-Yards)	64-341	50-248
Fumble Returns-Yards	0-0	0-0
Punt Returns-Yards	2-52	0-0
Kickoff Returns-Yards	4-50	5-42
Interception-Yards	0-0	1-24
Punts (Number-Yards)	3-105	5-196
Fumbles-Lost	1-0	0-0
Sacks By (Number-Yards)	2-11	1-7
Penalties-Yards	3-24	5-32
Possession Time	34:06	25:54

pass from Tafralis to John Broussard. San Jose attempted a two-point conversion of its own to extend the lead to three points. The conversion failed despite a second try because of defensive holding by BSU linebacker Colt Brooks on the first attempt.

San Jose's momentum carried over to the next kickoff. BSU was flagged for a block in the back, which pushed the Broncos back to their own six-yard line. Things only got worse for BSU as Zabransky was intercepted on the next play of the game. Spartan cornerback Chris Owens picked off Zabransky's pass and returned it 24 yards to the BSU five-yard line.

San Jose scored three plays later on a three-yard touchdown pass from Tafralis to Jones.

Boise State's offense went back to work with a 20-12 deficit and just 10:38 to play in the fourth quarter. BSU comprised a 12-play, 63-yard drive, which was capped off by a one-yard Zabransky touchdown run. Zabransky found Jerard Rabb on the two-point conversion, which tied the score 20-20. The catch was one of just two for Rabb in the game, but it couldn't have come at a more opportune time.

"I think we're starting to get more and more confident with (Zabransky) and the receivers," Rabb said. "He's starting to leave it up there for us to make plays."

The BSU defense held strong on the final San Jose offensive possession of the game. The Broncos forced the Spartans into a third and three from their own 40-yard line. On third down Tafralis went to his main target, James Jones, one last time. Jones had caught eight passes for 88 yards and two touchdowns in the game up to

Ian Johnson picks up yardage against the San Jose State defense. *Stanley Brewster/Arbiter*

that play. However, Jones failed to hold on to what would have been his ninth catch, just past the first-down marker.

On the next play Tadman sprung the big punt return that propelled BSU to its 10th win of the season. Tadman led the defense in tackles with seven, including one for a nine-yard loss on San Jose's first drive of the game.

Ian Johnson continued his dominating play. He finished with 151 rushing yards on 29 carries and one touchdown. Zabransky started for BSU despite an illness that kept him out of Friday's

workouts at Spartan Stadium. Zabransky finished the game 14-21 for 181 yards.

"He's only got so many games left as a Bronco and there was no doubt he'd be out there battling," Petersen said.

After the game Johnson was taken to a local hospital. He was complaining of nausea. He was expected to be fine.

The Broncos play their final home game of the season Saturday November 18 against Utah State.

SENIORS SHINE FOR BOISE STATE

BY DREW MAYES

In what could be his last game at Bronco Stadium, senior quarterback Jared Zabransky was nearly perfect, completing 21-of-23 passes for 236 yards and three touchdowns. Zabransky and 22 other seniors led Boise State (11-0, 7-0 Western Athletic Conference) past Utah State (1-10, 1-6) 49-10 in dominating fashion.

Zabransky was just one of many seniors to come up big for the Broncos. Running back Brett Denton started in place of injured Heisman hopeful Ian Johnson, who is still suffering the effects of a partially collapsed lung he suffered in last week's 23-20 win over San Jose State. With Denton carrying the load, the Bronco running game picked up an impressive 264 yards on the ground.

Denton scored for the Broncos on the team's first two possessions of the game. The first came on a three-yard rush up the middle and the second on a 27-yard scamper that saw Denton follow three lead blocks into the heart of the Aggie defense. Denton finished the game with 125 rushing yards and two touchdowns.

Utah State's offense on the other hand could get nothing going early on—going three-and-out in each of its first three possessions.

The Broncos offense remained hot. Zabransky completed 18 passes in a row. He went 5-for-5 during Boise State's third offensive drive, including a 47-yard laser to fellow senior Jerard Rabb for the touchdown and a comfortable 21-0 lead.

Broncos wide receiver Jovan Hutchinson celebrates his 10-yard touchdown reception on a pass from backup quarterback Taylor Tharp.

Stanley Brewster/Arbiter

"I didn't realize it was 18 in a row," Zabransky said after the game. "It just felt like I was in a rhythm out there."

Leon Jackson came in at quarterback for Utah State, relieving an ineffective Riley Nelson. Jackson drove the Aggies down the field into Bronco territory, including a long 43-yard pass to Kevin Robinson. The drive would stall at the Bronco 22-yard line. The Aggies turned the ball over on downs.

Two plays later, the Broncos would cough up the ball to Utah State. Vinny Perretta fumbled, giving the Aggies the ball in Bronco territory. The turnover would cost Boise State three points. Bryan Shields hit a 31-yard field goal to cut the Bronco lead to 21-3.

Any momentum the Aggies were gaining was quickly lost when Zabransky found another senior receiver in the end zone for a touchdown. This time it was Legedu Naanee on a 15-yard score with more than a minute left in the half to give the Broncos a comfortable 28-3 halftime lead.

Boise State picked up in the second half right where they left off in the first. The Broncos marched down the field and scored when Quinton Jones rushed off the left side for an eight-yard touchdown. Jones, arguably the team's fastest player, had seen very little action at running back this year. The senior spent much of the season as the team's starting cornerback on defense.

The Aggie offensive struggles continued in the second half with Nelson back behind center. The freshman quarterback was intercepted by Bronco senior safety Marty Tadman, also playing in his final game on the Blue.

Three plays later Zabransky found his senior tight end Ryan Putnam in the end zone for an eight-yard touchdown and a 42-3 Bronco lead to end the third quarter.

With the big lead and great day behind him, Zabransky would leave the game early, giving the offensive reins to backup quarterback Taylor Tharp. The offense looked to score again with Tharp under center, but he was sacked by Aggie linebacker Paul Igboeli.

Tharp fumbled on the sack, which was recovered by Utah State's Devon Hall, who took the ball 64 yards in the opposite direction for the defensive touchdown.

The score was too little, too late for the Aggies.

The Broncos put the icing on their senior day cake when Tharp found seldom-used senior receiver Jovan Hutchinson in the corner of the end zone for a 10-yard touchdown. The touchdown was the first of Hutchinson's four-year career at Boise State and sealed the Broncos' 49-10 victory.

"It's so much emotion (the touchdown catch)—the hard work, sweat and tears," Hutchinson said. "I've struggled with playing time and injuries here for five years."

The outstanding play of many of the team's seniors was not lost on their defensive leader, Korey Hall.

Boise State receiver Legadu Naanee (4) takes advantage of a great block as he heads for the end zone.
Stanley Brewster/Arbiter

	1st	2nd	3rd	4th	Final
Utah State	0	3	0	7	10
Boise State	14	14	14	7	49

Scoring Summary

1st

BSU: Denton 3-yard run (Montgomery kick)—10 plays, 75 yards in 4:54.

BSU: Denton 27-yard run (Montgomery kick)—5 plays, 62 yards in 1:23.

2nd

BSU: Rabb 46-yard pass from Zabransky (Montgomery kick)—7 plays, 84 yards in 3:18.

USU: Shields 31-yard field goal—9 plays, 32 yards in 3:36.

BSU: Naanee 16-yard pass from Zabransky (Montgomery kick)—3 plays, 30 yards in 1:15.

3rd

BSU: Jones 8-yard run (Montgomery kick)—9 plays, 63 yards in 4:33.

BSU: Putnam 8-yard pass from Zabransky (Montgomery kick)—3 plays, 49 yards in 0:42.

4th

USU: Hall 64-yard fumble recovery (Shields kick)

BSU: Hutchinson 10-yard pass from Tharp (Montgomery kick)—12 plays, 70 yards in 6:50.

Team Statistics

	USU	**BSU**
First Downs	7	24
Rushing Yards (Net)	90	231
Passing Yards (Net)	98	257
Passes (Comp-Att-Int)	9-19-1	25-27-0
Total Offense (Plays-Yards)	49-188	68-488
Fumble Returns-Yards	1-64	0-0
Punt Returns-Yards	1-4	2-30
Kickoff Returns-Yards	8-134	3-54
Interception-Yards	0-0	1-7
Punts (Number-Yards)	6-254	2-99
Fumbles-Lost	0-0	3-2
Sacks By (Number-Yards)	1-13	2-8
Penalties-Yards	6-44	6-66
Possession Time	26:38	33:22

"When you think of senior day, this is what you think about," Hall said. "All the seniors getting in and making a play."

Not only does the win keep the dreams of a Bowl Championship Series game alive for the Broncos, it guarantees at least a share of its fifth consecutive Western Athletic Conference title. Boise State can win the WAC title outright with a victory at Nevada.

However, all the championships and potential BCS game talk were taking a backseat to the team's performance November 18, particularly the play of its seniors.

"There was something special on that field today," Rabb said.

For the 22 seniors playing in their last regular-season game at Bronco Stadium—indeed there was.

The Broncos celebrate with Brett Denton (35) after one of Denton's two first-quarter rushing touchdowns.
Stanley Brewster/Arbiter

BRONCOS STOMP WOLF PACK

BY DUSTIN LAPRAY

Exhale.

You can do it now. You can relax and bask in the splendor of an undefeated season.

The Boise State Broncos defeated the Nevada Wolf Pack 38-7 November 25 in Reno to win their fifth consecutive Western Athletic Conference Championship and finish the season 12-0, 8-0 WAC.

Last season, the Broncos shared the WAC title. This year, it's all theirs.

"We didn't want to share it," BSU tailback Ian Johnson said.

"We wanted to be outright champions. One of the worst things in the world last year was being on the plane and having someone tell you, 'Hey, you guys eeked into being WAC champions because someone else lost.' We wanted to be outright, 100 percent champions."

Johnson was carried off the field by a mass of fans who rushed the field after the win. He also set the school record for single-season rushing yards on a three-yard touchdown run in the fourth quarter. Johnson broke Brock Forsey's 2002 record of 1,611 yards. Johnson currently has 1,613.

He rushed for 147 yards on 31 carries at Nevada.

Johnson crossed the end zone three times in the game, bringing his season touchdown total to 24. He still leads the nation in that category.

The Broncos truly dominated the game. They only allowed the Nevada offense to tally 141 total yards. The Broncos allowed a season-low 35

Ian Johnson stays a step ahead of Nevada's Nick Hawthorne. Johnson had three touchdowns against the Wolf Pack.
Stanley Brewster/Arbiter

passing yards. Jeff Rowe, Nevada's senior quarterback, completed 6-of-15 passes. He threw zero interceptions and zero touchdowns.

"I thought our defense was unbelievable," BSU head coach Chris Petersen said. "I don't think I've ever seen them more dominating in a game than they were today."

The Broncos were focused, prepared.

"We watched so much tape on those guys," Petersen said. "By the end of the year you see how they play. They've got good players and they have a good program. They've moved the ball the last five games. The combination of how their defense was playing … not in my wildest dreams would I expect them to play a game like that."

The Broncos shut out the Wolf Pack in the first half.

Nevada didn't pick up its first first down until the 6:12 mark of the second quarter. The Bronco defense held Nevada to 18 first-quarter yards and forced three turnovers.

Marty Tadman recovered a Robert Hubbard fumble, forced by Orlando Scandrick, in the second quarter and returned it to the Wolf Pack 16-yard line.

Drisan James evades Nevada's Scott Garrison for extra yardage. *Stanley Brewster/Arbiter*

"WE WATCHED SO MUCH TAPE ON THOSE GUYS…NOT IN MY WILDEST DREAMS WOULD I EXPECT THEM TO PLAY A GAME LIKE THAT."

BSU HEAD COACH
CHRIS PETERSEN

Tadman's recovery led to the first Bronco points, a 27-yard field goal by Anthony Montgomery.

Coach Petersen could have given Montgomery other opportunities in the first half, but opted to go for first downs deep in Nevada territory. The Broncos went 1-for-4 on fourth-down conversions in the first half, turning the ball over on downs on their first two possessions.

"I wasn't going to come out in this game and play conservative and all that," Petersen said. "I really wanted to go for it there. Nevada, credit their defense; they stopped us a few times on fourth and short there. That's uncommon for us to get stopped there. I didn't have any regrets at all."

Jared Zabransky had another solid game at quarterback for BSU. The senior threw for 299 yards on 20-of-27 passing and one long, beautiful bomb to Legedu Naanee, a 45-yard score.

Naanee caught seven balls for 129 yards and the score.

Zabransky threw one interception. It proved costly (Nevada senior Nick Hawthrone returned it 45 yards for a score), but since the Nevada offense was as effective as a one-legged man in an ass-kicking contest, it really didn't matter.

Johnson got off to a slow start, only rushing for nine yards in the first quarter and 40 in the first half. Johnson capped an 11-play, 72-yard drive at 12:03 of the second quarter with a six-

	1st	2nd	3rd	4th	Final
Boise State	3	14	14	7	38
Nevada	0	0	7	0	7

Scoring Summary

1st

BSU: Montgomery 28-yard field goal—4 plays, 5 yards in 1:31.

2nd

BSU: I. Johnson 6-yard run (Montgomery kick)—11 plays, 72 yards in 4:33.

BSU: I. Johnson 4-yard run (Montgomery kick)—1 play, 4 yards in 0:14.

3rd

BSU: Perretta 5-yard run (Montgomery kick)—10 plays, 80 yards in 4:47.

BSU: Naanee 45-yard pass from Zabransky (Montgomery kick)—4 plays, 57 yards in 2:00.

NEV: Hawthrone 45-yard interception return (Jaekle kick).

4th

BSU: I. Johnson 3-yard run (Montgomery kick)—11 plays, 80 yards in 6:21.

Team Statistics

	BSU	NEV
First Downs	25	4
Rushing Yards (Net)	178	106
Passing Yards (Net)	299	35
Passes (Comp-Att-Int)	20-27-1	6-15-0
Total Offense (Plays-Yards)	79-477	37-141
Fumble Returns-Yards	1-13	0-0
Punt Returns-Yards	4-16	1-15
Kickoff Returns-Yards	0-0	7-144
Interception-Yards	0-0	1-45
Punts (Number-Yards)	2-90	7-276
Fumbles-Lost	1-0	5-4
Sacks By (Number-Yards)	4-26	3-13
Penalties-Yards	5-41	7-55
Possession Time	37:48	22:12

yard run. He later scored on a 4-yard run, following Nevada quarterback Jeff Rowe's fumble on a scramble. Officially the force was given to Andrew Browning.

Browning went nuts in the game. He led the team with seven tackles from his defensive tackle position. He had four tackles for a loss, for 25 yards, three sacks and the forced fumble.

Vinny Perretta also scored another touchdown, a five-yard keeper to the left side.

Korey Hall also had seven tackles to lead the team.

"We knew this was one of our biggest games because of the situation and nobody was going to take that away from us," Hall said. "We've been working for this for five years and we put it all together finally. We had to work for it. It is a great feeling, accomplishing our goals."

The goals the team set at the beginning of the season are complete, but now, with the undefeated season and a Bowl Championship Series game looming on the Arizona horizon, there is a new goal, to win the upcoming game, wherever it may be, whoever they will play.

Nevada will probably earn a berth in the MPC Computer Bowl in Boise. They finished the season 8-4, 5-3 WAC. They will face a team from the Atlantic Coast Conference.

Josh Bean (56), Ian Johnson (41), coach Chris Petersen and the rest of the team celebrate their probable invitation to the Tostitos Fiesta Bowl after defeating Nevada. *Stanley Brewster/Arbiter*

HALL STANDS TALL, THE BEDROCK BRONCO

BY DUSTIN LAPRAY

Korey Hall is a small-town kid. But he is a big-time linebacker for the Boise State Broncos. The senior mike backer led the Broncos in 2006 in tackles (105) and interceptions (6).

He was recently named the Western Athletic Conference Defensive Player of the Year for the 2006 season.

He was named First-Team All-WAC for the third year in a row, a quarterfinalist for the Lott Trophy, was named the Broncos' most outstanding defensive player, and moved into fourth place on BSU's all-time tackles list. He finished with double-digit tackles four times in the regular season.

He helped lead his team to the Tostitos Fiesta Bowl, one of the Bowl Championship Series bowls.

That's quite a lot for a kid from Glenns Ferry, Idaho. The town lies on the Snake River in southwest Idaho. It is a rural community, its namesake based on an actual man who ferried settlers across the Snake in their quest to find opportunity in the west.

Opportunity.

The word is key when talking of this stalwart young man. He grasped his opportunity, one of his only shots at playing college football, when he signed with the BSU program.

Hall was a stud at Glenns Ferry High School, where he played both linebacker and running back. He recorded 359 tackles in his four years as a starter in the 2A division. He also rushed for 2,802 yards. In these smaller schools, the athletes are asked to do so much more than they do in larger schools. Hall also played special teams and placed second in the Idaho State Wrestling Tournament his senior year.

Hall fit right in when he came to Boise State. His work ethic and blue-collar mentality jelled quite naturally with the hard-nosed Broncos. He was and still is willing to do anything for his team.

His savvy pass coverage has let him record more interceptions (11) than any other linebacker in WAC history.

And now, in his final game as a Bronco, his future on the line, desires for a career in construction management in his future and every

Korey Hall runs the ball after an interception versus Oregon State.
Stanley Brewster/Arbiter

Korey Hall moves in for a tackle against the Wyoming Cowboys.
Stanley Brewster/Arbiter

media member in Phoenix wondering how he and his Broncos will do in the Fiesta Bowl, Hall is as composed as ever. He is calm and focused and ready to show the nation what he and his defense can do, not only on the Blue, but on the Phoenix Green too.

"You gotta go into the game the same as you would every other game," Hall said. "If we can stick with what's been working with us all season, we'll be alright."

But there are doubters out there questioning the mid-major Broncos' ability to hang with the class of the NCAA and its most-hailed tailback, Adrian Peterson.

"He's obviously one of the best running backs in the nation and we're going to have to try to contain him," Hall said. "I think that's the key to us winning. If we can come in and stop the run, we're going to have a chance to be successful. I think going into any football game, if you can run the ball and stop the other team from running the ball on you, you have a chance to be successful and that's what we're going to try to do."

The Broncos have done quite well this season slowing down the run and in many instances, straight up negating opposing offenses from any rushing success. The Broncos

"YOU GOTTA GO INTO THE
GAME THE SAME AS YOU
WOULD EVERY OTHER GAME.
...IF WE CAN STICK WITH
WHAT'S BEEN WORKING
WITH US ALL SEASON, WE'LL
BE ALRIGHT."

BOISE STATE LINEBACKER
KOREY HALL

rank No. 18 nationally in scoring defense, ironically one slot behind the Oklahoma Sooners. With Hall as its captain, the Bronco defense is No. 7 in the nation in rush defense, giving up about 98 yards per game on the ground. Stopping the run puts opposing offenses into third-and-long situations and forces them to make mistakes or punt the ball away.

"We want to control the game, the ball, create turnovers, and not give them up," Hall said.

And that is a sound goal. But most of the nation isn't giving these Broncos a chance. For Hall, he has been fighting for a chance for years. He has been playing for respect and playing to play and all those things which make the Idaho athlete so pure.

"Our team and definitely our senior class, we have a chip on our shoulder," Hall said. "We want to come out and show people what we're all about and that we have a great team."

The 12-0 Broncos will be tested in this Fiesta Bowl. Hall and his teammates will have a chance to prove whether or not they truly belong among the elites of college football. To beat the best, you must be the best, at least for one day. That day is the first of 2007, a new year and another opportunity for this small-town man.

FIESTA BOWL BITTERSWEET FOR CAVENDER BROTHERS

BY DREW MAYES

For Jeff and Pete Cavender, the experience of the Fiesta Bowl has been a little bittersweet.

The twin brothers had been playing football together every year since they were in fourth grade, but that all changed this past summer when Pete ruptured his Achilles tendon during summer conditioning drills. The injury forced Pete to miss the entire 2006 season and separated the brothers on the field for the first time ever.

> "IT SAYS CAVENDER ON THE BACK OF MY JERSEY, BUT THAT'S NOT JUST MY LAST NAME, IT'S HIS TOO. IT'S IMPORTANT TO HIM AND IT'S IMPORTANT TO MYSELF THAT I REPRESENT BOTH OF US OUT THERE."
>
> BOISE STATE RIGHT GUARD
> JEFF CAVENDER

"I knew exactly what happened as soon as it happened," Pete said. "The injury is just another hurdle I have to climb over. I think he's [Jeff] taken the injury harder than I have."

In honor of his twin brother, Jeff dedicated this season to his brother by wearing his number, 64, throughout the year.

Jeff Cavender (64) leads the Broncos out to the field against New Mexico State.
Stanley Brewster/Arbiter

Jeff Cavender (64) protects Jared Zabransky (5) as he attempts to make a pass.

Stanley Brewster/Arbiter

"It says Cavender on the back of my jersey, but that's not just my last name, it's his too," Jeff said. "It's important to him and it's important to myself that I represent both of us out there."

The significance of his brother's gesture did not go unnoticed or unappreciated by Pete.

"COMING TO BOISE STATE I DIDN'T EVEN DREAM OF PLAYING IN A BCS GAME"

BOISE STATE RIGHT GUARD JEFF CAVENDER

"It's pretty cool recognition from him and shows you what kind of guy he is," Pete said. "It put a pretty big lump in my throat the first time I saw it."

While Pete continues to progress in rehabilitation ahead of schedule, his brother Jeff is about to start his 37th consecutive game as a Bronco this Monday against Oklahoma in the biggest game either of the brothers have played in.

"Coming to Boise State I didn't even dream of playing in a BCS game," Jeff said.

Jeff probably didn't dream of playing three different positions in three years for the Broncos either, but that hasn't stopped the standout lineman from completing the offensive lineman trifecta. His freshman year, Jeff started all 12 games as the team's right tackle. Last year he started every game as center and this year as right guard.

While Jeff continues to set the standard for Bronco offensive linemen, his brother continues to contribute to the team any way he can despite his Achilles injury.

"I try to keep as busy as I can helping out, and Coach Kugler has done a great job of letting me help him," Pete said. "It's kept me motivated, gave me a purpose this season, and made me feel like part of this team."

While the 2006 season has provided very different experiences for the Cavenders, both agree they'll be looking forward to doing what is necessary for the Broncos to have another successful year in 2007—together.

BOISE STATE WINS FIESTA BOWL 43-42

BY JAKE GARCIN

The biggest game in Boise State history quickly became the greatest game ever played by the program Monday night. In just over four hours the world learned that all the hype surrounding the BSU football program was for real. With 2:40 left in the Tostitos Fiesta Bowl, Boise State and Oklahoma engaged in one of the most unforgettable last-minute shootouts in college football history. And with 73,719 fans on the edge of their seats in the University of Phoenix Stadium, the Broncos scored on a two-point conversion to ink their names down in the history books.

For 52 minutes the Broncos led the Sooners in a game that provided a fast start, a steady middle, and a hectic finish. After jumping out to a 14-0 lead seven and a half minutes into the game, BSU controlled the scoreboard until 1:26 left in regulation.

Sooner quarterback Paul Thompson found Quentin Chaney for a 5-yard touchdown pass to cap off a 7-play, 77-yard drive that only took 1:14 to culminate. Trailing 26-28 and having no timeouts left, the Sooners had no choice but to go for a two-point conversion to tie the game.

On the two-point conversion attempt Oklahoma tried to utilize the size mismatch between Chaney (6-foot-5, 208 lbs.) and BSU cornerback Orlando Scandrick (5-foot-11, 187 lbs.). Scandrick was flagged for pass interference after getting locked up with Chaney on a fade route to the back left corner of the end zone. On the ensuing retry Thompson connected with Jermai Gresham for the

Ian Johnson dances into the end zone for the game-winning two-point conversion in overtime.
Stanley Brewster/Arbiter

score, only to have an illegal shift called against the Sooners, setting up a third two-point conversion attempt. Thompson finally found Juaqu Iglesias in the middle of the end zone to even the score at 28-28 and set up an expected overtime session to decide the outcome of the game.

Boise State did have more than a minute of clock left to work with, and as the Broncos took over at their own 25-yard line it was apparent they had no intentions of playing conservatively. The aggressive approach backfired as Jared Zabransky was intercepted on the first play of the drive by OU's Marcus Walker, who returned the pick 35 yards for a touchdown and a 35-28 lead.

As the Boise State offense slumped off the field, BSU head coach Chris Petersen and staff began preparing for one last push to steal back a missed opportunity at overtime. With just 1:02 left in the game Zabransky stepped back under center and found senior tight end Derek Schouman on a 36-yard strike. The Broncos hurried to the line of scrimmage and ran a no-huddle snap as the clock ran down under 0:45 left to play. The OU defense penetrated the Bronco backfield however, and Zabransky was sacked for a loss at the 50-yard line, forcing BSU to use its second timeout of the half.

On second down Jerard Rabb failed to come down with a toss from Zabransky. With a third-and-18 play on the line, Zabransky watched as a pass sailed off the hands of senior wide receiver Drisan James. The Broncos faced a fourth and 18 with 22 seconds left and their undefeated season on the line. BSU offensive coordinator Bryan Harsin called for the only play Boise State fans had seen this year and wouldn't expect to see again; the hook and ladder.

BSU had run, and scored on, the hook and ladder against Idaho earlier in the season. This time Zabransky hit James across the middle of the field, at which point James pitched the football backwards to a streaking Jerard Rabb. Rabb hit the sideline and turned on the after burners, diving across the goalline to pull the Broncos within a point with :07 left in the game. An Anthony Montgomery field goal tied the game at 35-35, finally securing an extra session of football.

"When he called it I was like let's go, let's go and get this done," James said about Coach Harsin calling for the hook and ladder play. "Little did I know that Rabb would be wide open down the sidelines. It felt pretty good."

Boise State won the coin toss to start overtime and elected to play defense against the Sooners first. With the ball on the 25-yard line, Oklahoma star running back Adrian Peterson bounced outside for a touchdown run on the first play of overtime. BSU had managed to hold Peterson to 52 rushing yards prior to the run, which was the only time all year Peterson was kept under the century mark in a game.

Facing its second deficit of the night, Boise State retook the field, looking to contrive one last miracle sequence. The Broncos went to Schouman three times on their first overtime drive, completing two-yard, 10-yard, and five-yard passes to the tight end.

Legedu Naanee forces the ball forward against the Sooners.
Stanley Brewster/Arbiter

	1	2	3	4	OT	Final
Boise State	14	7	7	7	8	43
Oklahoma	7	3	7	18	7	42

Scoring Summary

1st

BSU: James 49-yard pass from Zabransky (Montgomery kick)—7 plays, 71 yards in 3:40.

BSU: I. Johnson 2-yard run (Montgomery kick)—2 plays, 9 yards in 0:57.

OU: Johnson 8-yard pass from Thompson (Hartley kick)—14 plays, 82 yards in 6:54.

2nd

OU: Hartley 31-yard FG—5 plays, 38 yards, in 2:48.

BSU: James 32-yard pass from Zabransky (Montgomery kick)—6 plays, 65 yards in 1:19.

3rd

BSU: Tadman 27-yd. interception return (Montgomery kick)

OU: Peterson 8-yard run (Hartley kick)—2 plays, 11 yards in 0:47.

4th

OU: Hartley 28-yard FG. 8 plays—50 yards in 11:43.

OU: Chaney 5-yard pass from Thompson (Iglesias 2-pt. pass from Thompson)—6 plays, 77 yards in 1:14.

OU: Walker 33-yard interception return (Hartley kick)

BSU: Rabb 35-yard pass from Zabransky (Montgomery kick)—5 plays, 78 yards in 0:00.

Overtime

OU: Peterson 25-yard run (Hartley kick)—1 play, 25 yards.

BSU: Schouman 5-yard pass from Perretta (I. Johnson 2-pt. rush)—7 plays, 25 yards.

Team Statistics

	BSU	OU
First Downs	16	23
Rushing Yards (Net)	110	174
Passing Yards (Net)	267	233
Passes (Comp-Att-Int)	20-30-1	19-32-3
Total Offense (Plays-Yards)	65-377	70-407
Fumble Returns-Yards	0-0	0-0
Punt Returns-Yards	3-16	4-27
Kickoff Returns-Yards	6-124	6-85
Interceptions-Yards	3-52	1-33
Punts (Number-Yards)	8-333	5-202
Fumbles-Lost	2-2	1-1
Sacks By (Number-Yards)	2-13	3-16
Penalties-Yards	8-63	6-35
Possession Time	26:48	33:12

The final pass came on a half-back pass, which began by splitting Zabransky out of the backfield, direct snapping the ball to Vinny Perretta, running Perretta to the right, and finally throwing the ball to the back of the end zone to Schouman. Schouman finished the game with eight receptions for 72 yards and one touchdown.

"This is better than a dream," Schouman said after the game. "I got my number called a lot. I'm just glad I was getting those opportunities. For our school it's just a huge, exciting game, and I'm glad that we won."

The score pulled BSU within a point once again and confronted the team with its second compromising decision of the night, playing to win or playing for overtime. Despite the misfortune when going for the jugular once before, Coach Petersen called his offensive squad back onto the field to go for the two-point conversion and the win.

On the final play of the game Boise State called for the Statue of Liberty play, which left Ian Johnson with a gaping hole to jaunt into the end zone for the win. Zabransky pump faked to the right side of the field then handed the ball behind his back to Johnson who ran into the left side of the end zone for the go-ahead score. Johnson threw the football up into the crowd as the celebration began in the blue and orange section of the University of Phoenix stadium.

"They're so big, strong and physical, the first overtime didn't go so well," Petersen said about deciding to go for two. "One play, they were in the end zone. We like the play we had for a two-point conversion. It really wasn't a difficult decision at that point."

116

Gerald Alexander (2) jumps for a catch as Marty Tadman watches (20). *Stanley Brewster/Arbiter*

Following the game Boise State players celebrated with friends in the stands and hugged teammates on the field. Zabransky was awarded the Offensive Player of the Game award for his 19-29, 262-yard performance. Marty Tadman won the Defensive Player of the Game trophy after intercepting Thompson twice (once for a touchdown) to go along with five tackles. Despite one of his best games of the season, Tadman's defensive efforts were nearly overshadowed by the final three minutes of football.

"I have a pretty strong faith in God," Tadman said. "I think he has a strong will for us. I think he blessed us tonight. [I'm] very thankful and humbled by that. You also don't want to talk about the plays I didn't make. I'm happy to talk about the two I did."

For those who witnessed the 2007 Fiesta Bowl, it will certainly be a game not easily forgotten. The game was touted as the biggest one in school history and exceeded even the loftiest of expectations. The Broncos finished the season 13-0, with the final piece of the puzzle accounted for and complete.

LIKE HIS CAREER AT BSU, Z'S FINAL GAME IS ROLLER-COASTER RIDE

BY DREW MAYES

They say legacies are built on longevity, but for Bronco quarterback Jared Zabransky, his legacy may very well be defined in one game. In what will go down as the biggest game in the history of the Boise State football program, Zabransky finally got his first bowl game win and took home the game's offensive Most Valuable Player in Boise State's 43-42 overtime win against the University of Oklahoma.

"You know, this was an unbelievable game," Zabransky said. "This probably goes down in the history of college football, it can be argued as the best game ever."

Zabransky, a three-year starter, replaced Ryan Dinwiddie as the Broncos' starting quarterback as a sophomore. Replacing Dinwiddie was no small feat, as the former Bronco shattered school records and left as the NCAA all-time leader in passing efficiency.

After a sensational sophomore year in which Zabransky led the Broncos to an undefeated regular season, the kid from a potato farm in Hermiston, Oregon, was anointed as the golden boy of Bronco football. But a 44-40 loss against Louisville in the Liberty Bowl that ended on an interception in the end zone, followed by an opening season loss to Georgia in which Zabransky committed six first-half turnovers before being benched, changed the public's perception.

In less than a year the Bronco quarterback had gone from golden boy to whipping boy. Members of the media publicly called the quarterback out for his refusal

After struggling throughout his junior year, Jared Zabransky leads the team as a senior.
Stanley Brewster/Arbiter

to talk about the Georgia game. Boise State fans booed Zabransky at the end of the MPC Bowl when what looked to be an impressive Bronco comeback ended with another Zabransky interception. Zabransky was now 0-2 in bowl games, both of which ended with interceptions in the end zone that could have won the game.

The now-senior quarterback came into the 2006 season with many fans calling for his head. Instead of looking over his shoulder, Zabransky responded by having his best season statistically and leading the Broncos to another undefeated regular season and their first Bowl Championship Series appearance against the University of Oklahoma in the Tostitos Fiesta Bowl.

Taking a 21-10 lead into halftime, Zabransky looked every bit the mistake-free senior quarterback he had been all season, going 10-for-16 for 142 yards and two touchdowns.

But when the Sooners started to roll in the third quarter and the Bronco offense began falling stagnate, the questions of Zabransky in pressure situations once again became a hot topic for the fans in the stands and members of the media in the press box.

The talk intensified when Oklahoma tied the game 28-28 and took the lead one play later when Zabransky was intercepted by OU's Marcus Walker, who went 33 yards in the opposite direction for the touchdown to give the Sooners a 35-28 lead with just 1:02 left.

Zabransky would finish the game 19 of 29 for 262 yards and three touchdowns with one interception.

For the third straight year, Zabransky had thrown a costly interception in bowl game.

However, this time he would get one more chance.

"A minute with two timeouts is a lot of time," Zabransky said. "Anything can happen in a college football game and we knew that."

With the game and his legacy on the line, Zabransky had just one minute to define himself. Will he be remembered as the guy who consistently choked in pressure situations, or as the guy who led the Broncos to their first BCS victory? One minute to decide.

Sliding to his left to avoid the Sooner defenders, Zabransky started answering the question by finding tight end Derek Schouman for 36 yards over the middle to the OU 42.

Dropping back on the next play, Zabransky was sacked. What else would you expect at this point?

Two plays later, two incomplete passes.

Facing fourth down, Jared Zabransky had one play left to define himself.

One play, one player's legacy.

Needing to pick up 18 yards to sustain the drive, Zabransky found Drisan James for a 15-yard completion. Looking like the drive had come up just short, James lateralled the ball back to Jerard Rabb. Rabb turned on the jets, leaving Oklahoma defenders confused and grasping as the Bronco receiver went the remaining 35 yards for the game-tying touchdown.

"That's what a fifth-year senior quarterback needs to do to pull out a big win … it says a lot about him," Boise State head coach Chris Petersen said of Zabransky's play in the final drive. "The guy is a winner, check his record … he's as good as any quarterback in the country."

Down by seven in overtime, Zabransky went 2-for-2 in overtime and went in motion, drawing the attention of the OU defense as the Broncos directly snapped the ball to backup running back Vinny Perretta, who threw to Schouman in the end zone for the touchdown on fourth and two.

Instead of settling for the extra point to send the game into double overtime, the Broncos went for the win and a two-point conversion, putting the biggest game in the school's history in the hands of Zabransky.

In shotgun formation, Zabransky faked a screen pass to his right and handed the ball off to running back Ian Johnson, who sprinted his way into the end zone for the two-point conversion and the Bronco upset victory.

"He's learned a lot of hard lessons through the years, which all great quarterbacks do, and I think the biggest thing he learned is it's never over … you always have a chance," Petersen said.

"I'm so happy for my guys, this is an unbelievable game," Zabransky said. "After I threw that interception I had probably 10 guys come up to me and say there's a minute left … you can do it, and we did it."

After three years, Jared Zabransky had finally done it. He had finally won a bowl game as the Broncos starting quarterback. He had finally answered the critics.

After intercepting the ball twice, Marty Tadman wins Defensive Player of the Game.
Stanley Brewster/Arbiter

BRONCO WIN PROVES JOYOUS AND PAINFUL

BY JESSICA CHRISTENSEN

Keith Stein Blue Thunder Marching Band Director David Wells was immediately rushed to the emergency room after an alleged heart attack following the game. Current treatment and vitals are not known at this time.

Also following the game, Bronco running back Ian Johnson proposed to his girlfriend, Christine Popadics, just before the trophy announcement. Popadics, of Boise, attends Boise State and is a member of the Bronco Spirit Squad. Fellow football players had heard rumors of the proposal, but weren't sure when it would take place.

Johnson mentioned the proposal to Fiesta Bowl officials and they gave him the idea to propose after a "game-winning touchdown." He proposed immediately following that very thing.

"Right after the touchdown I waited for the cameras, surprised the hell out of her," Johnson said.

"I'm in shock, this was all too much. The game was enough," Popadics said.

Laughter was shared at the press conference as Bronco quarterback Jared Zabransky shared his thoughts on the proposal.

"I doubt it would have been as romantic if we had lost," Zabransky said.

Other members of the spirit squad and football players embraced both Johnson and Popadics as information of the proposal spread. Popadics stood outside the swarm of reporters around Johnson after the game.

Bronco safety Marty Tadman mentioned later in the press conference he wasn't surprised at the spontaneity of the proposal given Johnson's personal character.

After an emotional victory, Ian Johnson proposes to his girlfriend, Christine Popadics.
AP Images

INDIVIDUAL STATS (as of November 26, 2006)

Scoring	TD	FGs	PAT Kick	PAT Rush	PAT Rcv	PAT	Pass Points
Ian Johnson	24	0-0	0-0	0-0	0	0-0	144
Anthony Montgomery	0	13-14	56-58	0-0	0	0-0	95
Legedu Naanee	6	0-0	0-0	0-0	0	0-0	36
Jared Zabransky	6	0-0	0-0	0-0	0	1-3	36
Vinny Perretta	5	0-0	0-0	0-0	0	0-0	30
Brett Denton	4	0-0	0-0	0-0	0	0-0	24
Jerard Rabb	3	0-0	0-0	0-0	1	0-0	20
Derek Schouman	3	0-0	0-0	0-0	0	0-0	18
Drisan James	2	0-0	0-0	0-0	0	0-0	12
Quinton Jones	2	0-0	0-0	0-0	0	0-0	12
Jon Helmandollar	1	0-0	0-0	0-0	0	0-0	6
Jovan Hutchinson	1	0-0	0-0	0-0	0	0-0	6
Brad Lau	1	0-0	0-0	0-0	0	0-0	6
Ryan Putnam	1	0-0	0-0	0-0	0	0-0	6
Jeremy Childs	1	0-0	0-0	0-0	0	0-0	6
Colt Brooks	1	0-0	0-0	0-0	0	0-0	6
Marty Tadman	1	0-0	0-0	0-0	0	0-0	6
Orlando Scandrick	0	0-0	0-0	0-0	0	0-0	2
Kyle Stringer	0	0-0	0-0	1-1	0	0-0	2
Total	62	13-14	56-58	1-1	1	1-3	473
Opponents	25	5-10	20-20	0-1	1	1-4	187

TOTAL OFFENSE	G	PLAYS	RUSH	PASS	TOTAL	AVG/G
Jared Zabransky	12	348	189	2325	2514	209.5
Ian Johnson	11	253	1613	0	1613	146.6
Brett Denton	12	70	348	0	348	29.0
Vinny Perretta	12	53	314	0	314	26.2
Legedu Naanee	12	8	90	0	90	7.5
Taylor Tharp	6	17	-12	88	76	12.7
Drisan James	12	7	54	0	54	4.5
Jon Helmandollar	8	14	47	0	47	5.9
Brad Lau	11	7	28	0	28	2.5
Jerard Rabb	12	1	9	0	9	0.8
Bush Hamdan	4	3	4	4	8	2.0
Quinton Jones	11	3	1	0	1	0.1
Anthony Montgomery	12	1	-2	0	-2	-0.2
TEAM	6	7	-9	0	-9	-1.5
Total	12	792	2674	2417	5091	424.2
Opponents	12	688	984	2301	3285	273.8

RUSHING	GP	ATT	GAIN	LOSS	NET	AVG	TD	LONG	AVG/G
Ian Johnson	11	253	1651	38	1613	6.4	24	59	146.6
Brett Denton	12	69	364	16	348	5.0	3	27	29.0
Vinny Perretta	12	53	322	8	314	5.9	3	25	26.2
Jared Zabransky	12	89	334	145	189	2.1	6	24	15.8
Legedu Naanee	12	7	94	4	90	12.9	0	35	7.5
Drisan James	12	7	54	0	54	7.7	0	25	4.5
Jon Helmandollar	8	14	50	3	47	3.4	1	9	5.9
Brad Lau	11	7	31	3	28	4.0	0	13	2.5
Jerard Rabb	12	1	9	0	9	9.0	0	9	0.8
Bush Hamdan	4	1	4	0	4	4.0	0	4	1.0
Quinton Jones	11	3	11	10	1	0.3	1	8	0.1
Anthony Montgomery	12	1	0	2	-2	-2.0	0	0	-0.2
TEAM	6	7	0	9	-9	-1.3	0	0	-1.5
Taylor Tharp	6	4	8	20	-12	-3.0	0	4	-2.0
Total	12	516	2932	258	2674	5.2	38	59	222.8
Opponents	12	323	1245	261	984	3.0	5	48	82.0

PASSING	GP	EFFIC	COMP-ATT-INT	PCT	YDS	TD	LNG	AVG/G
Jared Zabransky	12	161.89	172-259-7	66.4	2325	20	61	193.8
Taylor Tharp	6	151.48	11-13-1	84.6	88	1	20	14.7
Bush Hamdan	4	66.80	1-2-0	50.0	4	0	4	1.0
Legedu Naanee	12	0.00	0-1-0	0.0	0	0	0	0.0
Brett Denton	12	0.00	0-1-0	0.0	0	0	0	0.0
Total	12	159.54	184-276-8	66.7	2417	21	61	201.4
Opponents	12	114.19	208-365-17	57.0	2301	15	65	191.8

RECEIVING	GP	NO.	YDS	AVG	TD	LONG	AVG/G
Legedu Naanee	12	34	522	15.4	6	61	43.5
Drisan James	12	33	554	16.8	2	56	46.2
Jerard Rabb	12	33	507	15.4	3	46	42.2
Derek Schouman	11	21	204	9.7	3	30	18.5
Vinny Perretta	12	16	121	7.6	2	33	10.1
Jeremy Childs	12	14	152	10.9	1	33	12.7
Brett Denton	12	7	76	10.9	1	24	6.3
Ryan Putnam	12	6	77	12.8	1	27	6.4
Ian Johnson	11	6	51	8.5	0	21	4.6
Brad Lau	11	5	36	7.2	1	12	3.3
Tanyon Bissell	9	2	29	14.5	0	20	3.2
Richie Brockel	11	2	20	10.0	0	12	1.8
Jovan Hutchinson	3	2	14	7.0	1	10	4.7
Julian Hawkins	4	1	42	42.0	0	42	10.5
Nick Harris	3	1	6	6.0	0	6	2.0
Jared Hunter	4	1	6	6.0	0	6	1.5
Total	12	184	2417	13.1	21	61	201.4
Opponents	12	208	2301	11.1	15	65	191.8

PUNT RETURNS	NO.	YDS	AVG	TD	LONG
Marty Tadman	14	128	9.1	0	44
Quinton Jones	13	132	10.2	0	20
Jeremy Childs	2	0	0.0	0	0
Kyle Wilson	1	3	3.0	0	0
Drisan James	1	7	7.0	0	7
Total	31	270	8.7	0	44
Opponents	18	193	10.7	1	64

KICK RETURNS	NO.	YDS	AVG	TD	LONG
Quinton Jones	20	403	20.1	0	36
Rashaun Scott	6	117	19.5	0	42
Drisan James	1	17	17.0	0	17
Total	27	537	19.9	0	42
Opponents	64	1197	18.7	1	93

FUMBLE RETURNS	NO.	YDS	AVG	TD	LONG
Marty Tadman	1	13	13.0	0	13
Total	1	13	13.0	0	13
Opponents	1	64	64.0	1	64

INTERCEPTIONS	NO.	YDS	AVG	TD	LONG
Korey Hall	6	108	18.0	0	41
Marty Tadman	4	149	37.2	1	98
Colt Brooks	2	12	6.0	1	12
Quinton Jones	2	78	39.0	1	61
Orlando Scandrick	1	25	25.0	0	25
Gerald Alexander	1	0	0.0	0	0
Kyle Wilson	1	16	16.0	0	16
Total	17	388	22.8	3	98
Opponents	8	185	23.1	2	56

FIELD GOALS	FGM-FGA	PCT	01-19	20-29	30-39	40-49	50-99	LG	BLK
Anthony Montgomery	13-14	92.9	0-0	5-5	7-8	1-1	0-0	40	0

PUNTING	NO.	YDS	AVG	LONG	TB	FC	I20	BLKD
Kyle Stringer	39	1764	45.2	61	6	5	8	1
TEAM	1	0	0.0	0	0	0	0	0
Total	40	1764	44.1	61	6	5	8	1
Opponents	67	2730	40.7	64	5	7	14	0

KICKOFFS	NO.	YDS	AVG	TB	OB	RETN	NET	YDLN
Anthony Montgomery	72	4268	59.3	13	0			
Kyle Stringer	14	844	60.3	3	0			
Total	86	5112	59.4	16	0	1197	41.8	23
Opponents	39	2223	57.0	7	2	537	39.6	25

OVERALL DEFENSIVE STATS	GP	SOLO (TACKLES)	AST (TACKLES)	TOTAL	TFL/YDS	(SACKS) NO-YDS	(PASS) INT-YDS	BRUP	QBH	(FUMBLES) RCV-YDS	(FUMBLES) FF	BLOCKED KICKS
Korey Hall	12	54	51	105	6-5-25	3-5-19	6-108	1	1	1-0	-	-
Marty Tadman	12	35	27	62	1-5-10	-	4-149	1	-	1-13	1	-
Colt Brooks	12	28	24	52	8-0-36	6-5-27	2-12	2	-	1-0	2	-
Kyle Gingg	11	22	28	50	4-0-17	2-5-14	-	2	-	1-0	1	-
Orlando Scandrick	12	29	17	46	5-5-25	2-0-12	1-25	5	-	-	2	1
Nick Schlekeway	12	9	33	42	4-0-9	1-5-4	-	1	-	2-0	-	-
Dennis Ellis	12	17	24	41	3-5-25	2-0-21	-	-	-	-	-	-
Andrew Browning	12	20	20	40	10-0-50	8-0-45	-	-	-	-	1	1
David Shields	12	19	20	39	5-0-9	-	-	1	-	-	-	-
Gerald Alexander	12	23	10	33	-	-	1-0	3	-	1-0	1	-
Kyle Wilson	9	23	8	31	0-5-0	-	1-16	5	-	1-0	1	-
Quinton Jones	11	21	4	25	0-5-0	-	2-78	5	-	-	-	-
Josh Bean	11	6	12	18	-	-	-	-	-	1-0	-	-
Mike T.Williams	11	9	9	18	5-5-28	3-0-18	-	1	-	-	-	-
Austin Smith	9	8	5	13	-	-	-	1	-	1-0	1	-
Ellis Powers	9	5	7	12	-	-	-	-	-	-	-	-
Ia Falo	12	7	5	12	-	-	-	-	-	-	-	-
Phillip Edwards	7	4	6	10	2-0-14	1-0-11	-	-	-	-	-	-
J.B. Van Hoogen	9	8	2	10	-	-	-	-	-	-	-	-
Mike G. Williams	12	1	9	10	0-5-2	-	-	-	-	-	-	-
Tim Brady	9	4	6	10	-	-	-	-	-	-	-	-
Rashaun Scott	9	2	5	7	-	-	-	-	-	-	-	-
Garrett Tuggle	7	4	3	7	-	-	-	1	-	-	-	-
Tristan Patin	5	5	-	5	-	-	-	-	-	-	-	-
Mike Dominguez	11	4	1	5	1-5-5	1-0-5	-	-	-	-	-	-
Tanyon Bissell	9	2	3	5	-	-	-	-	-	-	-	-
Joe Bozikovich	3	1	3	4	1-0-2	-	-	-	-	-	-	-
Sean Bingham	4	-	3	3	0-5-1	-	-	-	-	-	-	-
Ian Smart	10	-	3	3	-	-	-	-	-	-	-	-
Dallas Dobbs	6	2	1	3	1-0-1	-	-	-	-	-	-	-
Jon Helmandollar	8	1	1	2	-	-	-	-	-	-	-	-
Vinny Perretta	12	-	2	2	-	-	-	-	-	-	-	-
Nick Harris	3	2	-	2	-	-	-	-	-	-	-	-
Jadon Dailey	12	1	-	1	-	-	-	-	-	-	-	-
Ryan Clady	12	1	-	1	-	-	-	-	-	-	-	-
Evan Surratt	3	-	1	1	-	-	-	-	-	-	-	-
Tim Volk	2	-	1	1	-	-	-	-	-	-	-	-
Anthony Montgomery	12	-	1	1	-	-	-	-	-	-	-	-
Ian Johnson	11	1	-	1	-	-	-	-	-	-	-	-
Total	12	378	355	733	61-259	31-176	17-388	29	1	10-13	10	2
Opponents	12	-	-	-	-	17-126	8-185	23	6	9-64	13	1

TEAM STATS

	BSU	OPP
SCORING	473	187
Points Per Game	39.4	15.6
FIRST DOWNS	258	167
Rushing	145	50
Passing	101	106
Penalty	12	11
RUSHING YARDAGE	2674	984
Yards Gained Rushing	2932	1245
Yards Lost Rushing	258	261
Rushing Attempts	516	323
Average Per Rush	5.2	3.0
Average Per Game	222.8	82.0
TDs Rushing	38	5
PASSING YARDAGE	2417	2301
Att-Comp-Int	276-184-8	365-208-17
Average Per Pass	8.8	6.3
Average Per Catch	13.1	11.1
Average Per Game	201.4	191.8
TDs Passing	21	15
TOTAL OFFENSE	5091	3285
Total Plays	792	688
Average Per Play	6.4	4.8
Average Per Game	424.2	273.8
KICK RETURNS: #-YARDS	27-537	64-1197
PUNT RETURNS: #-YARDS	31-270	18-193
INT RETURNS: #-YARDS	17-388	8-185
KICK RETURN AVERAGE	19.9	18.7
PUNT RETURN AVERAGE	8.7	10.7
INT RETURN AVERAGE	22.8	23.1
FUMBLES-LOST	19-9	14-10

	BSU	OPP
PENALTIES-YARDS	68-585	82-645
Average Per Game	48.8	53.8
PUNTS-YARDS	40-1764	67-2730
Average Per Punt	44.1	40.7
Net Punt Average	36.3	35.2
TIME OF POSSESSION/GAME	31:49	28:11
3RD-DOWN CONVERSIONS	63/140	52/156
3rd-Down Pct	45%	33%
4TH-DOWN CONVERSIONS	15/19	10/19
4th-Down Pct	79%	53%
SACKS BY-YARDS	31-176	17-126
MISC YARDS	25	0
TOUCHDOWNS SCORED	62	25
FIELD GOALS-ATTEMPTS	13-14	5-10
ON-SIDE KICKS	0-0	0-3
RED-ZONE SCORES	59-66 89%	22-29 76%
RED-ZONE TOUCHDOWNS	47-66 71%	17-29 59%
PAT-ATTEMPTS	56-58 97%	20-20 100%
ATTENDANCE	182718	144222
Games/Avg Per Game	6/30453	6/24037

SCORE BY QUARTERS	1st	2nd	3rd	4th	Total
Boise State	118	159	112	84	473
Opponents	48	38	40	61	187

Stanley Brewster/Arbiter

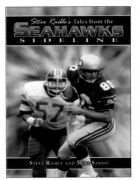
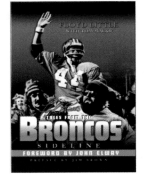
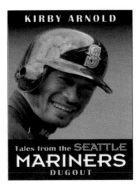
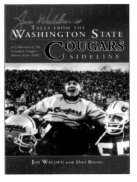
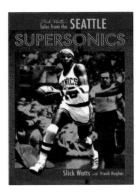
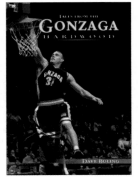